Workbook

for

Critical Thinking

by

Richard L. Epstein

Cartoons by Alex Raffi

Wadsworth Publishing Company
I(T)P® An International Thomson Publishing Company

Belmont, CA • Albany, NY • Bonn • Boston • Cincinnati • Detroit • Johannesburg • London
Madrid • Melbourne • Mexico City • New York • Paris • Singapore • Tokyo • Toronto • Washington

Philosophy Editor: *Peter Adams*
Editorial Assistant: *Kelly Bush*
Development Editor: *Alan Venable*
Marketing Manager: *David Garrison*
Assistant Editor: *Kerri Abdinoor*
Permissions Editor: *Robert Kauser*
Cover Design: *Stephen Rapley*
Signing Representative: Kim Johnson

For more information, contact Wadsworth Publishing Company,
10 Davis Drive, Belmont, CA 94002, or electronically at
http://www.thomson.com/wadsworth.html

International Thomson Publishing Europe
Berkshire House 168–173
High Holborn
London, WC1V 7AA, England

Thomas Nelson Australia
102 Dodds Street
South Melbourne 3205
Victoria, Australia

Nelson Canada
1120 Birchmount Road
Scarborough, Ontario
Canada M1K 5G4

International Thomson Publishing GmbH
Königswinterer Strasse 418
53227 Bonn, Germany

International Thomson Editores
Campos Eliseos 385, Piso 7
Col. Polanco
11560 México DF México

International Thomson Publishing Asia
60 Albert St.
50–01 Albert Complex
Singapore 189969

International Thomson Publishing Japan
Hirakawacho Kyowa Building, 3F
2–2–1–Hirakawacho
Chiyoda-ku, Tokyo 102, Japan

International Thomson Publishing Southern Africa
Building 18, Constantia Park
240 Old Pretoria Road
Halfway House, 1685 South Africa

ISBN 0-534-55840-2

A Living Dog is Better than a Dead Lion.

Ecclesiastes

Better than a live one, too.

Epstein

Workbook

for

Critical Thinking

by Richard L. Epstein

1   Critical Thinking?

Key Words

truth-value   conclusion
true   premise
false   critical thinking
claim   issue
argument

Exercises for Chapter 1

1. What's this course about?

2. How did I try to convince you in this book that this course is important? Can you pick out at least two *ways* I tried to convince you? Were they arguments?

3. Explain how to divide up all convincings depending on who is trying to convince whom.

4. Which of the following are claims?

   a.   Lassie is a dog.

   b.   I am 2 meters tall.

   c.   Is any politician not corrupt?

   d.   Power corrupts.

   e.   Feed Ralph.

   f.   Did you feed Ralph?

   g.   A friend in need is a friend indeed.

   h.   Why can't the English teach their children how to speak?

   i.   Strike three!

   j.   "Love is not love which alters when it alteration finds."

   k.   No se puede vivir sin amar.

   l.   Whenever Juney barks, Ralph gets mad.

   m. Wayne Newton lives in Las Vegas.

   n.   You believe that Wayne Newton lives in Las Vegas.

   o.   If the author of this book teaches in Las Vegas, then he lives in Nevada.

   p. $2 + 2 = 5$

   q.   I feel cold today.

   r. $\int_{1}^{7} \frac{1}{t} \, dt \;=\; \ln 7$

   s.   There is an odd number of stars in the universe.

5. Write down five sentences, four of which are claims and one of which is not. Exchange with a classmate and see if he or she can spot which are the claims.

6. How did I try to convince you that my definition of "claim" is a good definition?

7. What is the goal of an argument?

8. What is an argument?

9. What is a premise? What is a conclusion?

10. Why is not every attempt to convince you an argument? Give an example.

11. Give two examples of arguments that you have encountered outside class in the last two days.

12. Bring in a short article from the front page of a newspaper. Are all the sentences used in it claims? Is it an argument?

Here are two samples of exercises done by Tom, along with my comments.

Sheep are the dumbest animals. If the one in front walks off a cliff, all the rest will follow him. And if they get rolled over on their backs, they can't right themselves.

    Argument? (yes/no) Yes.

    Conclusion: Sheep are the dumbest animals.

    Premises: If a sheep walks off a cliff, all the rest will follow him.

                  If a sheep gets rolled over on its back, it can't right itself.

    This is good work, Tom.

How can you go to the movies with Sarah and not me? Don't you remember I helped you fix your car last week?

    Argument? (yes/no) Yes.

    Conclusion: You should go to the movie with me.

    Premises: I helped you fix your car last week.

Is what you are given an argument? No: There are just two questions, and questions aren't claims. So it can't be an argument. And if there's no argument, there are no premises and no conclusion. I grant that it seems we ought to interpret what he's saying as an argument—as you have done. But before we go putting words in someone's mouth, we ought to have rules and a better understanding of when that's justified.

13. You liked that movie? Boy are you dumb. I guess you just can't distinguish bad acting from good. And the photography was lousy. What a stupid ending, too.
      Argument? (yes/no)
      Conclusion:

      Premises:

14. Cats are nasty. They smell bad, they urinate in the house, they kill songbirds, they cause allergies so your friends can't come over. Why not just get a piece of wool with a recorder in it that will "miaou" when you stroke it?
      Argument? (yes/no)
      Conclusion:

      Premises:

15. If it's O.K. to buy white mice to feed a pet boa constrictor, why isn't it O.K. to buy white mice for your cat to play with?
      Argument? (yes/no)
      Conclusion:

      Premises:

16. You shouldn't eat at Zee-Zee Frap's restaurant. I heard they did really badly on their health inspection last week.
      Argument? (yes/no)
      Conclusion:

      Premises:

17. If you don't take a course on critical thinking you'll always end up being conned, a dupe for any fast-talker, an easy mark for politicians. So you should take a course on critical thinking. You'd be especially wise to take one from the instructor you've got now—(s)he's a great teacher.
      Argument? (yes/no)
      Conclusion:
      Premises:

18. Whatever you do, you should drop the critical thinking course from the instructor you've got now. (S)he's a really tough grader, much more demanding than the other professors that teach that course. You could end up getting a bad grade.

      Argument? (yes/no)

      Conclusion:

      Premises:

19. (Advertisement for Roundup®, a herbicide) Using Roundup® in your backyard makes gardening easy as well as effective. That's what gardening experts such as zoo horticulturists have learned through years of using the product. Since it can be used in areas where kids and pets are going to play, gardening experts have a high comfort level in using Roundup® in areas from backyards to zoo habitats. That's because any Roundup® not used by the sprayed plant quickly binds to the soil and breaks down into naturally occurring elements.

      Roundup® works by preventing production of certain proteins, special only to plants, which are needed for growth. Extensive tests show that it will not move in or on the soil to affect nearby plants. So this spring and summer, do what many zoos do–use Roundup® to beautify your surroundings.   (© 1996 Monsanto Company)

      Argument? (yes/no)

      Conclusion:

      Premises: (Just circle them.)

20. Look Dick! Look Zoe! See Spot. See Spot run.

      Argument? (yes/no)
      Conclusion:
      Premises:

21. Bad dog, bad dog. Jump over this fence again I'll get a newspaper and hit you.
      Argument? (yes/no)
      Conclusion:

      Premises:

22 Zoe: I don't love you.

     Dick: Don't be ridiculous. Of course you do. Why just yesterday you said you couldn't live without me. What would you do without me?
      Argument? (yes/no)

Conclusion:

Premises:

23. Letter to the editor:

Recently, there was an article in The Spectrum concerning pets being poisoned by anti-freeze. If this were intentional, what an awful thing to do. I do wonder about the owners of these pets. Why have you allowed your pets to wander the neighborhood unleashed in the first place? Most pets are considered a member of the family. If you cared at all for these animals, why are they allowed to run in the streets to be hit by a passing vehicle? While driving through my neighborhood early one morning, I almost hit three dogs because they ran up to my car barking.

Pet owners need to take responsibility for their animals. Not only is it unsafe for these pets to wander, it is very inconsiderate to other neighbors. Many of us are tired of the end-less, nauseating piles we have to shovel from our lawns and dead flowers caused by dogs passing by. Children in our neighborhoods cannot walk to a friend's house to play for fear of aggressive dogs. Pets should be in a fenced yard or on a leash, not just to protect pets, not just out of consideration for your neighbors, but also because it is the law.

Claudia Empey, *The Spectrum*

Argument? (yes/no)

Conclusion:

Premises: (Just circle them.)

24. Homosexuality can't be hereditary: Homosexual couples can't reproduce, so genes for homosexuality would have died out long ago.

Argument? (yes/no)

Conclusion:

Premises:

25. Letter to the editor:

I'm 45, a mother and a postal worker. I also happen to be in a long-term relation-ship with a woman. We both work, pay taxes, vote, do volunteer work, and lead full, productive lives.

My partner Sara and I have been together for over four years and we formal-ized our lifetime commitment to each other in a ceremony several years ago. In a fair and non-discriminating society, we would be able to obtain the same benefits for each other that heterosexual Americans obtain when they marry.

I've worked for the postal service for 10 years, yet I can't obtain health insurance for Sara, nor can I use family leave to care for or be with her if she's ill, has had surgery or has been injured.

Heterosexual employees who are married or get married can get benefits for a spouse and any number of children, including adopted, foster and stepchildren.

Even when we have legal papers drawn up to protect our rights, property and relationships, it often takes lengthy and expensive court battles to get other people to honor our wishes and instructions. Sometimes we lose those battles, and some rights (like family health insurance coverage) we simply can't get.

No one should be surprised that we want the right to marry.

Kathy Worthington, *The Spectrum,* May 26, 1996

Argument? (yes/no)

Conclusion:

Premises: (Just circle them.)

26. You may own stocks or securities which are selling at a lower price than when purchased. Tax considerations might call for a sale of such securities in order to create a currently deductible tax loss. However, if it is desired to still own the securities while producing a tax loss, you can't just sell securities at a loss and then buy them right back. Any purchase of the same securities within 30 days before or after the sale negates any losses. To get around this restriction, you can purchase similar but not identical securities to the ones sold. Or, in the case of bonds, you can achieve the same result by making a swap through a brokerage house.

1994 Tax Guide for College Teachers

Argument? (yes/no)

Conclusion:

Premises: (Just circle them.)

27. Oven Light Bulb

The light bulb is located in the upper left corner of the oven. Before replacing the bulb, disconnect electric power to the range at the main fuse or circuit breaker panel or unplug the range from the electric outlet. Let the bulb cool completely before removing it. Do not touch a hot bulb with a damp cloth as the bulb will break.

To remove: Hold hand under lamp bulb cover so it doesn't fall when released. With fingers of same hand, firmly push down wire bail until it clears cover. Lift off cover. Do not remove any screws to remove this cover. Replace bulb with a 40-watt home appliance bulb.

To replace cover: Place cover into groove of lamp receptacle. Lift wire bail up to center of cover until it snaps into place. When in place, wire holds cover firmly. Be certain wire bail is not below depression in center of cover.

How to get the best from your range, Hotpoint

Argument? (yes/no)

Conclusion:

Premises: (Just circle them.)

28. Dr. E is out for a walk with his dog. He gets ahead of her, comes to a fork in the path and goes along one side of it. His dog comes up to the fork and runs down the wrong side looking for him. Soon she re-appears at the fork and runs down the other side after him. Is Dr. E's dog using an argument? Explain.

29. Your friend goes outside, looks up at the sky and sees it's cloudy. She returns home and gets her raincoat and umbrella. Is she engaged in an argument? Explain.

30. Bring an advertisement to class that uses an argument. State the premises and conclusion.

31. In order to choose good courses of action in our lives we need not only knowledge of the world and the ability to reason well, but what else?

32. You've seen some arguments. What do you think should be the definition of "good argument"?

Writing Lesson 1

Write an argument either for or against the following:

"Student athletes should be given special leniency when the instructor assigns course marks."

Your argument should be at most one page long.

2   What Are We Arguing About?

Key Words

vague sentence   ambiguous sentence
objective claim   definition
subjective claim   persuasive definition
drawing the line   good definition

Exercises for Section A

1. What does it mean to say a sentence is vague?

2. Give an example of a vague sentence someone tried to pass off to you as a claim.

3. Bring to class instructions on medication or instructions from your doctor. Are they too vague?

4. Which of the following are too vague to be considered claims? (You may have to suggest a context in which it is spoken.)
   a. John always gets irritable when it's cold outside.

   b. Margery is the best cook in this school.

c. Richard looks like he has a cold today.

d. Dogs are better pets than cats.

e. Public animal shelters should be allowed to sell unclaimed animals to laboratories for experimentation.

f. Tuition at state universities should cover the entire cost to the university of a student's education.

g. All unnatural sex acts should be prohibited by law.

h. All citizens should have equal rights.

i. People with disabilities are just as good as people who are not disabled.

j. Boy are you lucky to get a date with Jane. On a scale of 1 to 10, she's at least a 9.

k. Zoe has beautiful eyes.

l. Dog food is cheaper at Lin's grocery store than at Smith's grocery.

m. Alpo is cheaper at Lin's grocery store than at Smith's grocery.

n. Spot is a big dog.

o. Cholesterol is bad for you.

p. English should be the official language of the United States.

q. "I am not a liar." [spoken by Richard Nixon]

r. Parents should be held responsible for crimes their children commit.

5. If someone wants to debate a sentence that you think is too vague to be treated as a claim, what should you do?

6. All the following are vague, but are they too vague for their intended purpose?
    a. Waiter, take back this steak and cook it longer. I asked for it medium.

b.   You call this painting job done? Don't come back until you've got it right.

c.   (On a TV weather report) There's a good chance of rain tomorrow.

d.   (On a TV weather report) There's a 70% chance of rain tomorrow.

e.   (Doctor's instructions) Your health will improve if you get more exercise.

f.   Harmful if swallowed.

g.   (Patient to doctor) Every time I swallow I get a burning sensation in my throat.

7.

Comment on the possible ways we could take what the clerk is saying, depending on what standards you think she has.

8.   Find an advertisement that treats a vague sentence as a claim.

9.   Explain why horoscopes are vague. Does the same apply to weather forecasts?

10. What's wrong with the following attempt to convince?

Look officer, if I were going 36 in this 35 m.p.h. zone, you wouldn't have given me a ticket, right? What about 37? But 45 you would? Well, isn't that saying that the posted speed limit is just a suggestion? Or do you write the law on what's speeding?

11. What is an objective claim? What is a subjective claim?

12. a.   Give an example of a true objective claim.

    b.   Give an example of a false objective claim.

    c.   Give an example of a true subjective claim.

    d.   Give an example of a false subjective claim.

13. Explain why a sentence that is too vague to be taken as an objective claim might be acceptable as a subjective claim.

14. Classify the following as objective or subjective. In some cases you may have to imagine who is saying it and the context. Where possible, explain your answer in terms of the standards you imagine are being used.

    a.   Wool insulates better than rayon.

    b.   Silk feels better on your skin than rayon.

    c.   Pablo Picasso painted more oil paintings than Norman Rockwell.

    d.   Bald men are more handsome.

    e   All ravens are black.

    f.   Gorillas have opposable thumbs.

    g.   You intend to do your very best work in this course.

    h.   Murder is wrong.

    i.   Your answer to Exercise 3 in Chapter 1 of this book is wrong.

    j.   Demons caused Jeffrey Dahmer to cut up and cannibalize people.

    k.   (In a law court, said by the defense attorney) The defendant is insane.

l.   He's sick, he's got the flu.

m.   He's sick. How could anyone say something like that?

n.   (Said to the professor after grades come out) I deserve a B not a D.

o.   Suzy believes that the moon does not rise and set.

p.   Dick's dog is hungry.

q.   God exists.

15. Make up a list of five claims for your classmates to classify as objective or subjective.

16. a.   Give an example of someone treating an objective claim as if it were subjective.

    b.   Give an example of someone treating a subjective claim as if it were objective.

17.

    Is Zoe right? How should Dick respond?

18. Suppose you're talking with a friend and he says that abortion is wrong. You ask him what he means: Wrong according to the Bible? According to the Koran? . . . And he responds, "I mean just plain *wrong*. Not wrong according to some standard. Just wrong." How should you reply?

19. Bring to class two advertisements, one that uses only subjective claims and another that uses only objective claims.

20. Find one of the ten articles of the Bill of Rights that uses vague words and explain why the vague language is not bad.

21. Do you think that the proposed law described in the following is too vague? Explain.

    Yvette Melanson grew up in Brooklyn believing she was white and Jewish.

    It wasn't until last month that she learned she was one of the so-called "Lost Birds"–Indian children often taken illegally and adopted by white families from the 1950s to the 1970s. . . .

    Melanson and her twin brothers were whisked away from their parents' hogan by a public health nurse when they were two days old. . . .

    The (Navajo) tribe also believes that Melanson's story underscores the importance of the 1978 Indian Child Welfare Act, which is under attack in Congress. The House-passed version of the bill would remove child custody proceedings from tribal courts if the cases involve children whose birth parents did not maintain "significant social, cultural or political affiliations with the tribe."

    Tribes say the vague language could open the door for state courts to decide that some children are not "Indian enough," allowing them to be adopted by white families.

    Associated Press, June 2, 1996

22. A few years ago the National Football League allowed teams to challenge a referee's call by requiring a head referee to view an instant replay of a disputed call and make a final determination. A few years later that practice was discontinued. Once again whatever the referees on the field decide is the final call. Comment on this in terms of the distinction between objective and subjective standards.

Exercises for Section B

1. a. Can a claim be ambiguous?

   b. Can a claim be vague?

2. Decide whether each of the following sentences is a claim. If it is ambiguous, give at least two sentences corresponding to the ways it could be understood.

   a. Zoe saw the waiter with the glasses.

   b. I was invited to go to the movies a week ago.

   c. Americans bicycle thousands of miles every year.

   d. (Sign in laundromat) Customers are required to remove their clothes when the machine stops.

   e. That psychiatrist helps torture victims.

   f. Zoe is cold.

   g. The players on the basketball team had a B average in their courses.

   h. Herman Melville wrote Moby-Dick.

   i. The judge let him get away with murder.

    j.   This is a civilized nation.

3.   How much ambiguity can we tolerate in an argument?

4.   Give an example of an ambiguous sentence you've heard recently.

5.   Give an example of an ambiguous sentence from an advertisement. Is the use of ambiguity intentional? Misleading?

6.   Each of the following arguments depends on ambiguity or vagueness to sound convincing. Rewrite at least one of the sentences to eliminate the ambiguity.

    a.   Zoe says that nothing is better than an ice cream cone on a hot summer's day. It's a hot summer's day. So, I better give Zoe nothing rather than this ice cream cone.

    b.   In some places, golden eagles have used the same nesting site for hundreds of years. So golden eagles live longer than humans.

    c.   Dick to Zoe: Anything that's valuable should be protected. Good abs are valuable—you can tell that because everyone is trying to get them. A layer of fat will protect my abs. So I should continue to be 5 lbs. overweight.

d. Croesus: Should I wage war on the Persians?
    Oracle at Delphi: If Croesus should wage war against the Persians, a great
                         empire will be destroyed.
    So Croesus went to war against the Persians.   When he lost he returned.
    Croesus: You lied! I waged war against the Persians and I lost.
    Oracle at Delphi: So a great empire was destroyed.

7. Ambiguous sentences are sometimes classified by the way in which they are
    ambiguous.
    a. A sentence is *semantically ambiguous* if the various meanings we can assign to it
        arise because a word or phrase has two standard meanings. For example, "Dogs
        smell better than horses." The problem is with the word "smell." Give two
        examples from a newspaper or magazine of semantically ambiguous sentences.

    b. A sentence is *syntactically ambiguous* if the various meanings we can assign to it
        arise because of the placement of the words in the sentence. For example, "Police
        help torture victims." Is the word "torture" is used here as an adjective modifying
        "victims," or as a verb with "Police" as subject. Usually the ambiguity is syntactical
        if you can clear it up by the way you say the sentence out loud. Give two examples
        from a newspaper or magazine of sentences that are syntactically ambiguous.

Exercises for Section C

1. Which of the following are definitions? Which are persuasive definitions? Which are neither?

    a. "Dog" means "a canine creature that brings love and warmth to a human family."

    b. Domestic violence is any violent act by a spouse or lover directed against his or her partner within the confines of the home of both.

    c. A feminist is someone who thinks that women are better than men.

    d. A conservative, in politics, is one who believes that we should conserve the political structure and laws as they are as much as possible, avoiding change.

    e. A liberal is someone who wants to use your taxes to pay for what he thinks will do others the most good.

    f. Love is blind.

    g. Sexual intercourse is when a man and a woman couple sexually with the intent of producing offspring.

2. For each of the following, give both a definition and a persuasive definition:

    a. Cat litter box

    b. Spouse

    c. School cafeteria

3. For each of (a)–(d) replace "believes in" with other words that mean the same:

    a. Zoe believes in free love.

    b. Dick believes in God.

    c. Zoe believes in the Constitution.

    d. Zoe believes in herself.

4. What is a good definition?

5. Give *definitions* that make the following subjective claims objective. *Don't rewrite the sentences.*

    a. It's hot outside.

    b. Eating more than 100 grams of fat every day is unhealthy.

6. Why should we avoid persuasive definitions?

7. Give an example of a definition used in one of your other courses.

8. *Mother defends decision to let daughter fly plane*

    Jessica Dubroff's mother Friday defended her decision to allow her 7-year-old daughter to make the flight that ended in tragedy, saying "you've no idea what this meant to Jess."

    "She had a freedom which you can't get by holding her back." a crying Lisa Blair Hathaway told NBC's "Today" while cradling her 3-year-old daughter Jasmine.

    Jessica, in an effort to become the youngest person to fly cross-country, was killed Thursday when her single-engine plane crashed in driving rain and snow shortly after takeoff, barely missing a house. Her father and flight instructor also died.

    At the site of the crash in a commercial-residential section of north Cheyenne, an impromptu memorial was set up as people dropped off flowers, teddy bears and even framed poems. By this morning the pile of teddy bears had grown to a row about 3 feet long by 8 feet wide. Someone placed a yellow flower on the driveway where the airplane's tail section came to rest.

    "I did everything so this child could have freedom and choice and have what America stands for," Hathaway said. "Liberty comes from . . . just living your life, . . . I couldn't bear to have my children in any other position."

    Hathaway said that if children were forbidden to do anything unsafe, "they would be padded up and they wouldn't go anywhere. They wouldn't ride a bicycle. My God they wouldn't do anything."

Associated Press, 1996

Show how Ms. Hathaway's argument relies crucially on the use of vague words.

We've learned a lot about how to classify claims and what passes for a claim but isn't. Here are a few of Tom's attempts to do some exercises that use all the ideas we've learned in this chapter, along with my corrections. He's supposed to circle the terms that apply.

Dogs bark.

<u>claim</u>	subjective	ambiguous or too vague	
not claim	objective	definition	persuasive definition

Yes, it's a claim. But if it's a claim, then it has to be either objective or subjective.

Cats are nasty.

<u>claim</u>	<u>subjective</u>	<u>ambiguous or too vague</u>	
not claim	objective	definition	persuasive definition

No—if it's ambiguous or too vague, then it's not a claim. This is an example of a subjective claim.

Rabbits are the principal source of protein for dogs in the wild.

<u>claim</u>	subjective	ambiguous or too vague	
not claim	<u>objective</u>	<u>definition</u>	persuasive definition

No—if it's a definition it's not a claim. And this is not a definition—what word is it defining? Certainly not "rabbit."

Dogs are canines that bring warmth and love to a family.

claim	subjective	ambiguous or too vague	
<u>not claim</u>	objective	definition	<u>persuasive definition</u>

No. If it's a persuasive definition, then it is a claim—just masquerading as a definition.

For each of 9–19, underline which of the terms apply. More than one may apply.

9. Rats do not have tails longer than 37% of their body length.

claim	subjective	ambiguous or too vague	
not claim	objective	definition	persuasive definition

10. Marriage is the legal union of a man and a woman.

      claim   subjective   ambiguous or too vague

      not claim   objective   definition   persuasive definition

11. A mark of A in this course means you know how to parrot what the professor said.

      claim   subjective   ambiguous or too vague

      not claim   objective   definition   persuasive definition

12. Steffi Graf is the best female tennis player in history.

      claim   subjective   ambiguous or too vague

      not claim   objective   definition   persuasive definition

13. This candy bar has 45% less fat than the average of the 25 leading chocolate brands, to be exact.

      claim   subjective   ambiguous or too vague

      not claim   objective   definition   persuasive definition

14. China has the largest land mass of any single country.

      claim   subjective   ambiguous or too vague

      not claim   objective   definition   persuasive definition

15. I've already seen the movie *Splash*.

      claim   subjective   ambiguous or too vague

      not claim   objective   definition   persuasive definition

16. There are 13 planets in our solar system.

      claim   subjective   ambiguous or too vague

      not claim   objective   definition   persuasive definition

17. It's cold outside.

      claim   subjective   ambiguous or too vague

      not claim   objective   definition   persuasive definition

18. Though legalizing drugs could cut taxes, as McKenna suggests, they destroy brain cells.

      claim   subjective   ambiguous or too vague

      not claim   objective   definition   persuasive definition

19. Administrators have no hearts.

      claim   subjective   ambiguous or too vague

      not claim   objective   definition   persuasive definition

20. Definitions can be classified according to their purpose.

    a. A *stipulative definition* is one that is used to give a particular meaning to a familiar word. For example, suppose we define "dog" to mean "a domestic canine that barks." Then "All dogs bark" becomes true *by definition*. Give two examples of stipulative definitions.

    b. An *explanatory definition* has the purpose of making some concept clear that may simply not be well-known to someone. For example, a carburetor is a device that mixes air and gasoline to the proper proportions for ignition before injecting the mixture into the cylinder in an internal combustion engine. Find two explanatory definitions in your other textbooks.

    c. A *precising definition* has the purpose of making a very general or vague word precise. For instance, by "cold" let's understand "below freezing." Give two examples of precising definitions.

Writing Lesson 2

We know that before we begin deliberating we should make the issue precise enough that someone can agree or disagree. Vague or ambiguous sentences are not claims.

Make the following sentence sufficiently precise that you could debate it:

"Student athletes should be given special leniency when the instructor assigns co urse marks."

Your definition or explanation should be at most one page long. That's at most one page, not at least or exactly one page.

To give you a better idea of what you're expected to do, I've included Tom's homework, along with my comments. He's still struggling.

Tom Wyzyczy
Critical Thinking
Section 4
Writing Lesson 2

"All unnatural sex acts should be prohibited by law."

Before we can debate this we have to say what it means. I think that "unnatural sex act" should mean any kind of sexual activity that most people think is unnatural. And "prohibited by law" should mean there's a law against it.

You've got the idea, but your answer is really no improvement. You can delete the first sentence. And you can delete "I think". We can guess that because you wrote the paper.

Your proposed definition of "unnatural sex act" is too vague. It's reminiscent of the standard the U.S. Supreme Court uses to define obscenity: prevailing community standards. In particular, what do you mean by "sexual activity"? Does staring at a woman's breasts count? And who are "people"? The people in your church? Your neighborhood? Your city? Your state? Your country? The world?

Of course "legally prohibited" means there's a law against it. But what kind of law? A fine? A prison sentence? A penalty depending on severity of the offense? How do you determine the severity?

Mary Ellen has a better idea how to do the assignment.

Mary Ellen Zzzyzzx
Critical Thinking
Section 4
Writing Lesson 2

"All unnatural sex acts should be prohibited by law."

By "unnatural sex act" I shall mean any sexual activity involving genitals, consensual or not, *except* between a man and a woman who are both over sixteen and in a way that could lead to procreation if they wanted it to and which is unobserved by others.

By "prohibited by law" I shall mean it would be a misdemeanor comparable to getting a traffic ticket.

> *I don't really think that everything else is unnatural, but I couldn't figure out any other way to make it precise. Is that what we're supposed to do?   Mary Ellen*

You did just fine. Really, the burden to make it precise would be on the person suggesting the sentence be taken as a claim. Most attempts are going to seem like a persuasive definition. But at least you now have a claim you could debate. If the other person thinks it's the wrong definition, that would be a good place to begin your discussions.

---

3   What is a Good Argument?

Key Words

good argument   strong argument

plausible claim   weak argument

dubious claim   tests for an argument to be good

valid argument   begging the question

Exercises for Sections A–C

1. What is an argument?

2. What is a good argument?

3. What does it mean to say an argument is valid?

4. What does it mean to say an argument is strong?

5. If an argument is valid or strong, does that mean it is a good argument? Explain.

6. How can you show that an argument is not valid?

7. If an argument is valid and its premises are true, is its conclusion true, too? Explain.

8. If an argument is bad, what does that show about its conclusion?

9. If an argument is strong and its premises are true, is its conclusion true, too? Explain.

10. To be classified as good, an argument must pass three tests. What are they?

11. a.   Make up an example of an argument that is valid and good.

    b.   Make up an example of an argument that is valid and bad.

12. a.   Make up an example of an argument that is strong and good.

    b.   Make up an example of an argument that is strong and bad.

13. Make up an example of an argument that is weak.

14. Can we show that an argument is not valid by showing that its conclusion is false? Example or explanation.

15. To decide whether an argument is good, does it depend on whether it convinced anyone?

16. Can an argument be both valid and strong?

17. What do we call an argument with a false premise?

18. Which, according to the definitions we're using, are incorrect uses of "valid" or "invalid"? For incorrect ones, rewrite the sentence without that word.

   a. Tom has a valid reason for showing up late to football practice.

   b. That's not a valid excuse.

   c. Your parking sticker is invalid.

   d. That's not a valid answer to my question.

   e. Your reasoning is invalid.

   f. I can't believe the referee made that decision. It's completely invalid.

For exercises 19–24, circle the claim that makes the argument valid. (You're not supposed to judge whether the claim is plausible, just whether it makes the argument valid.)

19. The dogs are drinking a lot of water today. It must be hot.

    a.   Dogs always drink when they are hot.

    b.   Every dog will drink when the weather is hot.

    c.   Hot weather means dogs will drink.

    d.   Only on hot days do dogs drink a lot of water.

    e.   None of these.

20. Every color monitor I've had either was defective and had to be returned or else burned out in less than two years. So you'd be foolish to buy a color monitor.

    a.   You should do what I tell you to do.

    b.   Every color monitor will be defective or go bad.

    c.   All monitors that are reliable are not color.

    d.   None of the above.

21. Puff is a cat. So Puff meows.

    a.   Anything that meows is a cat.

    b.   Dogs don't meow.

    c.   All cats meow.

    d.   Most cats meow.

    e.   None of the above.

22. Spock is a Vulcan. So Spock doesn't feel emotion.

    a.   Vulcans aren't humans.

    b.   Humans can't spot Vulcan emotions.

    c.   No Vulcan has emotions.

    d.   Most Vulcans feel no emotion most of the time.

    e.   None of the above.

23. The President is on every channel on television. So he must be making an important speech.

    a.   Only Presidents make important speeches on television.

    b.   When the President makes an important speech on television, he's on every channel.

    c.   When the President is on every channel on TV, he's making an important speech.

    d.   Presidents only make important speeches.

    e.   None of the above.

24. If Spot gets into the garbage, Dick will hit him with a newspaper. So Dick hit Spot.

    a.   The garbage is a bad thing for Spot to get into.

    b.   Whenever Spot gets into the garbage, Dick hits him.

    c.   Whenever Dick hits Spot, Spot was in the garbage.

    d.   Spot got into the garbage.

    e.   None of the above.

25. In a civil case one person or company is attempting to collect damages from another. According to the instructions the judge gives in California,

    > The plaintiff has the burden of proving by a preponderance of the evidence all of the facts necessary to establish . . .

    "Preponderance of evidence" means:

    > Such evidence as, when weighed with that opposed to it, has more convincing force and the greater probability of truth.

    For a criminal case, the government must prove the issue of guilt beyond reasonable doubt. In the California Code "reasonable doubt" is defined:

    > It is not mere possible doubt; because everything relating to human affairs, and depending on moral evidence, is open to some possible or imaginary doubt. It is that state of the case, which, after the entire comparison and consideration of the evidence, leave the minds of jurors in that condition that they can not say they feel an abiding conviction, to a moral certainty, of the truth of the charge.

    a. Do these definitions give objective criteria for the jury? Explain.

    b. How would you rewrite these two definitions to put them on the scale from weak to strong as in the diagram above?

    c. In some trials of cases concerning mortgages, separate property in a marriage, naturalization questions, and others, a different standard of proof is required:

    > The plaintiff has the burden of proving by clear and convincing evidence.

    "Clear and convincing evidence" is understood in California as:

    > Clear, explicit and unequivocal; so as to leave no substantial doubt; sufficiently strong to command the unhesitating assent of every reasonable mind.

    How does this compare to the standards for criminal and civil cases?

Name _____ Section _____

Exercises for Chapter 3

1. Is it always better to make our arguments valid rather than strong? Explain.

2. Identifying the conclusion of an argument is important. Words like "therefore" or "so" indicate a conclusion is coming up. List at least five more words or phrases that we use to introduce a conclusion. List five words that indicate premises.

    conclusion

    premises

3. If an argument is bad, what does that tell us about the conclusion?

4. A mathematician suspects that an extremely abstruse mathematical claim is true. He isn't sure, but he decides to investigate its consequences. He finds after some investigation that using the claim as a premise he can prove that a well-known theorem of mathematics is false. What should he conclude?

5. If we want to give a good argument with a subjective claim as conclusion, would it be better for it to be valid or strong?

6. To prove an objective claim should we always give an argument that is valid? Explanation or example.

7. Which subjects in your school would employ only valid arguments? Which would employ primarily strong arguments? Which would rely on a mix of the two?

    valid only

    primarily strong

    mixture

We've learned a lot about how to classify arguments. Here are some of Tom's answers to exercises that require all the ideas we've learned in this chapter. He's supposed to answer the italicized questions. I've left my comments attached.

Ralph is a dog. So Ralph barks.

Argument? (yes or no) Yes.

Conclusion: Ralph barks.

Premises: Ralph is a dog.

Classify: <u>valid</u>   very strong ——————— weak

If not valid, show why:

Good argument? (check one)

    It's good (passes the three tests). √

    It's bad because a premise is false.

    It's bad because it's weak.

    It's bad because a premise is more dubious than the conclusion.

    It's valid or strong, but you don't know if the premises are true, so you can't say if it's good or bad.

No! This isn't valid. Ralph might be a basenji. But it's fairly strong, so a pretty good argument if the premise is true—which you don't know for sure.

Whenever Spot barks, there's a cat outside. Since he's barking now, there must be a cat outside.

Argument? (yes or no) Yes.

Conclusion: Whenever Spot barks, there's a cat outside.

Premises: Spot's barking now. There must be a cat outside.

Classify: valid   very strong ———X——— weak

If not valid, show why: Maybe he's barking because the garbageman's there.

Good argument? (check one)

    It's good (passes the three tests).

    It's bad because a premise is false.

    It's bad because it's weak. √

    It's bad because a premise is more dubious than the conclusion.

    It's valid or strong, but you don't know if the premises are true, so you can't say if it's good or bad.

No. The conclusion is: "There's a cat outside." Ask yourself where you could put "therefore" in the argument. Which claims are evidence for which others? The argument is valid. But the premise "Whenever Spot barks, there's a cat outside" is pretty implausible, if not downright false. As you point out, what about the garbageman? So it's not a good argument.

Alison is Kim's sister, so Alison and Kim have the same mom and dad.

Argument? (yes or no) Yes.

Conclusion: Alison and Kim have the same mom and dad.

Premises: Alison is Kim's sister.

Classify: valid   very strong ——————X– weak

If not valid, show why: One of them might be adopted. Or they are half-sisters.

Good argument? (check one)

It's good (passes the three tests).

It's bad because a premise is false.

It's bad because it's weak. √

It's bad because a premise is more dubious than the conclusion.

It's valid or strong, but you don't know if the premises are true, so you can't say if it's good or bad.

Good work!

Bob has worked as a car mechanic for twenty years. Anyone who works that long at a job must enjoy it. So Bob enjoys being a car mechanic.

Argument? (yes or no) Yes.

Conclusion: Bob enjoys being a car mechanic.

Premises: Bob has worked as a car mechanic for twenty years. Anyone who works that long at a job enjoys it.

Classify: valid   very strong ——————X– weak

If not valid, show why: Bob might not be able to get any other job.

Good argument? (check one)

It's good (passes the three tests).

It's bad because a premise is false.

It's bad because it's weak. √

It's bad because a premise is more dubious than the conclusion.

It's valid or strong, but you don't know if the premises are true, so you can't say if it's good or bad.

Wrong! The argument is <u>valid</u>. What you showed is that the second premise is false or at least very dubious. So the argument <u>is</u> bad, but not for the reason you gave.

For Exercises 8–34 answer the italicized questions.

8.   Your hair was long. Now it's short. So you must have got a hair cut.

Argument? (yes or no)

Conclusion:

Premises:

Classify: valid   very strong —————— weak

If not valid, show why:

Good argument? (check one)

     It's good (passes the three tests).

     It's bad because a premise is false.

     It's bad because it's weak.

     It's bad because a premise is more dubious than the conclusion.

     It's valid or strong, but you don't know if the premises are true, so you can't say if
        it's good or bad.

9.   All cars have wheels. My bicycle has wheels. Therefore, my bicycle is a car.

    Argument? (yes or no)

    Conclusion:

    Premises:

    Classify: valid   very strong ————————— weak

    If not valid, show why:

    Good argument? (check one)

       It's good (passes the three tests).

       It's bad because a premise is false.

       It's bad because it's weak.

       It's bad because a premise is more dubious than the conclusion.

       It's valid or strong, but you don't know if the premises are true, so you can't say if
          it's good or bad.

10. Intelligent students study hard. Zoe studies hard. So Zoe is intelligent.

    Argument? (yes or no)

    Conclusion:

    Premises:

    Classify: valid   very strong ————————— weak

    If not valid, show why:

    Good argument? (check one)

       It's good (passes the three tests).

       It's bad because a premise is false.

       It's bad because it's weak.

       It's bad because a premise is more dubious than the conclusion.

       It's valid or strong, but you don't know if the premises are true, so you can't say if
          it's good or bad.

11. Dogs bark. Spot barks. So Spot is a dog.

   Argument? (yes or no)
   Conclusion:

   Premises:

   Classify: valid   very strong ——————— weak
   If not valid, show why:

   Good argument? (check one)
       It's good (passes the three tests).
       It's bad because a premise is false.
       It's bad because it's weak.
       It's bad because a premise is more dubious than the conclusion.
       It's valid or strong, but you don't know if the premises are true, so you can't say if
           it's good or bad.

12. All cats meow. Puff is a cat. So Puff meows.

   Argument? (yes or no)
   Conclusion:

   Premises:

   Classify: valid   very strong ——————— weak
   If not valid, show why:

   Good argument? (check one)
       It's good (passes the three tests).
       It's bad because a premise is false.
       It's bad because it's weak.
       It's bad because a premise is more dubious than the conclusion.
       It's valid or strong, but you don't know if the premises are true, so you can't say if
           it's good or bad.

13. All licensed drivers in Utah have taken a driver's test. Dick has taken a driver's
   test in Utah. So Dick is a licensed driver in Utah.

   Argument? (yes or no)
   Conclusion:

   Premises:

   Classify: valid   very strong ——————— weak
   If not valid, show why:

Good argument? (check one)

It's good (passes the three tests).

It's bad because a premise is false.

It's bad because it's weak.

It's bad because a premise is more dubious than the conclusion.

It's valid or strong, but you don't know if the premises are true, so you can't say if it's good or bad.

14. No dog meows. Puff meows. So Puff is not a dog.

Argument? (yes or no)

Conclusion:

Premises:

Classify: valid   very strong ——————— weak

If not valid, show why:

Good argument? (check one)

It's good (passes the three tests).

It's bad because a premise is false.

It's bad because it's weak.

It's bad because a premise is more dubious than the conclusion.

It's valid or strong, but you don't know if the premises are true, so you can't say if it's good or bad.

15. No cat barks. Spot is not a cat. So Spot barks.

Argument? (yes or no)

Conclusion:

Premises:

Classify: valid   very strong ——————— weak

If not valid, show why:

Good argument? (check one)

It's good (passes the three tests).

It's bad because a premise is false.

It's bad because it's weak.

It's bad because a premise is more dubious than the conclusion.

It's valid or strong, but you don't know if the premises are true, so you can't say if it's good or bad.

16. All students who study hard are liked by their teachers. Zoe is liked by all her teachers. Therefore, Zoe studies hard.

    Argument? (yes or no)
    Conclusion:

    Premises:

    Classify: valid   very strong ——————— weak
    If not valid, show why:

    Good argument? (check one)
    It's good (passes the three tests).
    It's bad because a premise is false.
    It's bad because it's weak.
    It's bad because a premise is more dubious than the conclusion.
    It's valid or strong, but you don't know if the premises are true, so you can't say if it's good or bad.

17. Spot is a black and white dog. Therefore, Spot is a dog.

    Argument? (yes or no)
    Conclusion:

    Premises:

    Classify: valid   very strong ——————— weak
    If not valid, show why:

    Good argument? (check one)
    It's good (passes the three tests).
    It's bad because a premise is false.
    It's bad because it's weak.
    It's bad because a premise is more dubious than the conclusion.
    It's valid or strong, but you don't know if the premises are true, so you can't say if it's good or bad.

18.

Argument? (yes or no)
Conclusion:

Premises:

Classify: valid   very strong ———————— weak
If not valid, show why:

Good argument? (check one)
　　It's good (passes the three tests).
　　It's bad because a premise is false.
　　It's bad because it's weak.
　　It's bad because a premise is more dubious than the conclusion.
　　It's valid or strong, but you don't know if the premises are true, so you can't say if
　　　　it's good or bad.

19. Dick missed almost every basket he shot in the game. He couldn't run, he couldn't
jump. He should give up basketball.
Argument? (yes or no)
Conclusion:

Premises:

Classify: valid   very strong ———————— weak
If not valid, show why:

Good argument? (check one)
　　It's good (passes the three tests).
　　It's bad because a premise is false.
　　It's bad because it's weak.
　　It's bad because a premise is more dubious than the conclusion.
　　It's valid or strong, but you don't know if the premises are true, so you can't say if
　　　　it's good or bad.

20. All people who haven't gone to college are bad company. The students in this class
have gone to college. So no students in this class are bad company.
Argument? (yes or no)
Conclusion:

Premises:

Classify: valid   very strong ——————— weak
If not valid, show why:

Good argument? (check one)
    It's good (passes the three tests).
    It's bad because a premise is false.
    It's bad because it's weak.
    It's bad because a premise is more dubious than the conclusion.
    It's valid or strong, but you don't know if the premises are true, so you can't say if
       it's good or bad.

21.

Argument? (yes or no)
Conclusion:

Premises:

Classify: valid   very strong ——————— weak
If not valid, show why:

Good argument? (check one)
    It's good (passes the three tests).
    It's bad because a premise is false.
    It's bad because it's weak.
    It's bad because a premise is more dubious than the conclusion.
    It's valid or strong, but you don't know if the premises are true, so you can't say if
       it's good or bad.

22. What do you want to eat for dinner? Well, we had fish yesterday, and pasta the other day. We haven't eaten chicken for awhile. How about some chicken with potatoes?

Argument? (yes or no)

Conclusion:

Premises:

Classify: valid   very strong ——————— weak

If not valid, show why:

Good argument? (check one)

    It's good (passes the three tests).

    It's bad because a premise is false.

    It's bad because it's weak.

    It's bad because a premise is more dubious than the conclusion.

    It's valid or strong, but you don't know if the premises are true, so you can't say if it's good or bad.

23. Dick: I just heard you on the phone to the travel agent. What's up? I thought we were going to drive to San Francisco.

    Zoe: Look, your car's broken down twice in the last two weeks. It would be stupid to take it on a long trip to San Francisco.

Argument? (yes or no)

Conclusion:

Premises:

Classify: valid   very strong ——————— weak

If not valid, show why:

Good argument? (check one)

    It's good (passes the three tests).

    It's bad because a premise is false.

    It's bad because it's weak.

    It's bad because a premise is more dubious than the conclusion.

    It's valid or strong, but you don't know if the premises are true, so you can't say if it's good or bad.

24. Maria: Almost all the professors I've met at this school are liberals.

    Manuel: So to get a teaching job here it must help to be a liberal.

Argument? (yes or no)

Conclusion:

Premises:

Classify: valid   very strong ——————— weak
If not valid, show why:

Good argument? (check one)
    It's good (passes the three tests).
    It's bad because a premise is false.
    It's bad because it's weak.
    It's bad because a premise is more dubious than the conclusion.
    It's valid or strong, but you don't know if the premises are true, so you can't say if
       it's good or bad.

25. —Either Sam is a professor or he has learned a lot on his own from reading.
    —He's not a professor, he's a restaurant owner.
    —So Sam has learned a lot on his own.
    Argument? (yes or no)
    Conclusion:

    Premises:

    Classify: valid   very strong ——————— weak
    If not valid, show why:

    Good argument? (check one)
        It's good (passes the three tests).
        It's bad because a premise is false.
        It's bad because it's weak.
        It's bad because a premise is more dubious than the conclusion.
        It's valid or strong, but you don't know if the premises are true, so you can't say if
           it's good or bad.

26. Tom: If Dick bought a new car, he must have had more money than I thought.
    Harry: Well, look, there's the new hatchback he bought.
    Tom: So Dick must have had more money than I thought.
    Argument? (yes or no)
    Conclusion:

Premises:

Classify: valid   very strong ———————— weak
If not valid, show why:

Good argument? (check one)
    It's good (passes the three tests).
    It's bad because a premise is false.
    It's bad because it's weak.
    It's bad because a premise is more dubious than the conclusion.
    It's valid or strong, but you don't know if the premises are true, so you can't say if
        it's good or bad.

27. Suzy: Mary Ellen wasn't home last night when I called.
    Zoe: She said she was going to stay home last night to study.
    Suzy: She's been pretty interested in Harry. I bet she went out with him.

Argument? (yes or no)
Conclusion:

Premises:

Classify: valid   very strong ———————— weak
If not valid, show why:

Good argument? (check one)
    It's good (passes the three tests).
    It's bad because a premise is false.
    It's bad because it's weak.
    It's bad because a premise is more dubious than the conclusion.
    It's valid or strong, but you don't know if the premises are true, so you can't say if
        it's good or bad.

28. Suzy: Mary Ellen wasn't home last night when I called.
    Zoe: She said she was going to stay home last night to study.
    Suzy: She's been pretty interested in Harry. I bet she went out with him.
    Zoe: Do you really think so?
    Suzy: Sure. She's so serious about her studies. Only a good-looking guy could drag
        her away from her books.

Argument? (yes or no)

Conclusion:

Premises:

Classify: valid   very strong ——————— weak
If not valid, show why:

Good argument? (check one)
    It's good (passes the three tests).
    It's bad because a premise is false.
    It's bad because it's weak.
    It's bad because a premise is more dubious than the conclusion.
    It's valid or strong, but you don't know if the premises are true, so you can't say if
        it's good or bad.

29. Suzy: Mary Ellen wasn't home last night when I called.
    Zoe: She said she was going to stay home last night to study.
    Suzy: She's been pretty interested in Harry. I bet she went out with him.
    Zoe: Do you really think so?
    Suzy: Sure. She's so serious about her studies. Only a good-looking guy could drag
            her away from her books. And Harry told me he was planning to call her.
    Zoe: You're probably right. I talked with her mom this morning, and if there'd
            been some sort of emergency at her place, she would have said.
    Suzy: And Harry's the only guy she's even talked about in the last month.

Argument? (yes or no)
Conclusion:

Premises:

Classify: valid   very strong ——————— weak
If not valid, show why:

Good argument? (check one)

It's good (passes the three tests).
It's bad because a premise is false.
It's bad because it's weak.
It's bad because a premise is more dubious than the conclusion.
It's valid or strong, but you don't know if the premises are true, so you can't say if it's good or bad.

30. Every student who has ever taken a critical thinking course from this instructor has gotten an A. Therefore, I will get an A in this course.

Argument? (yes or no)
Conclusion:

Premises:

Classify: valid   very strong ———————— weak
If not valid, show why:

Good argument? (check one)

It's good (passes the three tests).
It's bad because a premise is false.
It's bad because it's weak.
It's bad because a premise is more dubious than the conclusion.
It's valid or strong, but you don't know if the premises are true, so you can't say if it's good or bad.

31. Dick was dressed. Now Dick is naked. So Dick removed his clothes.

Argument? (yes or no)
Conclusion:

Premises:

Classify: valid   very strong ———————— weak
If not valid, show why:

Good argument? (check one)

It's good (passes the three tests).
It's bad because a premise is false.
It's bad because it's weak.
It's bad because a premise is more dubious than the conclusion.
It's valid or strong, but you don't know if the premises are true, so you can't say if it's good or bad.

32. Your instructor was born. Therefore, your instructor will die.

    Argument? (yes or no)
    Conclusion:

    Premises:

    Classify: valid   very strong ——————— weak
    If not valid, show why:

    Good argument? (check one)
       It's good (passes the three tests).
       It's bad because a premise is false.
       It's bad because it's weak.
       It's bad because a premise is more dubious than the conclusion.
       It's valid or strong, but you don't know if the premises are true, so you can't say if
          it's good or bad.

33. No one will live forever. So your instructor will die.

    Argument? (yes or no)
    Conclusion:

    Premises:

    Classify: valid   very strong ——————— weak
    If not valid, show why:

    Good argument? (check one)
       It's good (passes the three tests).
       It's bad because a premise is false.
       It's bad because it's weak.
       It's bad because a premise is more dubious than the conclusion.
       It's valid or strong, but you don't know if the premises are true, so you can't say if
          it's good or bad.

34. There are 30 seconds left in the football game. The 49ers have 35 points. The
    Dolphins have 7 points. So the 49ers will win.

    Argument? (yes or no)
    Conclusion:

    Premises:

Classify: valid   very strong ——————— weak
If not valid, show why:

Good argument? (check one)
      It's good (passes the three tests).
      It's bad because a premise is false.
      It's bad because it's weak.
      It's bad because a premise is more dubious than the conclusion.
      It's valid or strong, but you don't know if the premises are true, so you can't say if
          it's good or bad.

Writing Lesson 3

We've been learning how to analyze arguments. Now it's time to try to write one.

You know what tests a good argument must pass. It must be composed of claims, and claims only. It shouldn't contain any vague or ambiguous sentences. It must be valid or strong, or at least as strong as the issue allows. And the premises should be plausible.

Write an argument either for or against the following:

"Everyone should use a bicycle as his or her main form of transportation."

Your argument should be at most one page long.
Just list the premises and the conclusion. Nothing more.
Check whether your instructor has chosen a *DIFFERENT TOPIC* for this assignment.

It doesn't matter if you never thought about the subject, or whether you think it's terribly important. This is an exercise, a chance for you to sharpen your skills in writing arguments. It's the process of writing an argument that should be your focus.

If you have trouble coming up with an argument, think how you would respond if you heard someone say the claim at a city council meeting or if someone in class said it. Make two lists: *pro* and *con*. Then write the strongest argument you can.

Don't get carried away. You're not expected to spin a one-page argument into three pages. You can't use any of the literary devices you've been taught are good fillers. List the premises and conclusion—that's all. And remember, premises and conclusion don't have those words "therefore" or "I think" attached. Once you can write an argument in this outline form, you can worry about making your arguments sound pretty. It's clarity we want first.

To give you a better idea of what you're expected to do, I've included Tom's argument on a different topic.

Tom Wyzyczy
Critical Thinking
Section 4
Writing Lesson 3

Issue: Students should be required to take a course on critical thinking.

Definition: I'll understand the issue as "College students should be required to take a course on critical thinking before graduating."

Premises:

A critical thinking course will help students to write better in their other courses.

A critical thinking course will help students to read assignments in all their other courses.

A critical thinking course will make students become better informed voters.

Most students who take a critical thinking course appreciate it.

Professors will be able to teach their subjects better if they can assume their students know how to reason.

Critical thinking is a basic skill and should be required, like Freshman Composition.

Conclusion: College students should be required to take a course on critical thinking before graduating.

Tom, it's good that you began by making the issue precise. Even better is that you realized the definition wasn't a premise. You've learned a lot from the last assignment.

Your argument is pretty good. You've used claims for your premises. Some of them are a bit vague. But only the fourth is so vague you should delete it or make it more precise. All of your premises support your conclusion. But the argument's not strong as stated. You're missing some glue, something to fill the gap. You're piling up evidence, but to what end? To your third premise, I'd just say "SO?" And you never used that you're talking about <u>college</u> students. Won't your argument work just as well for high school? Is that what you want?

We'll look at how to fill in what you've missed in the next chapter.

Writing Lesson 4

For each of the following write the best argument you can that has as conclusion the claim below the cartoon. List only the premises and conclusion. If you believe the best argument is only weak, explain why.

Do not make up a story about the cartoon—this isn't a course in creative writing. Use what you see in the cartoon and your common knowledge.

1.

Spot ran away.

2.

Spot chased a cat.

3.

Professor Zzzyzzx is cold.

4.

Dick should not drink the coffee.

4   Repairing Arguments

Key Words

unstated premise	indicator word
unstated conclusion	unrepairable argument
rationality	irrelevant claim
suspend judgment	imply
The Principle of Rational Discussion	infer
The Guide to Repairing Arguments	

Exercises for Sections A–D

1. Why add premises or a conclusion? Why not take arguments as they are?

2. State the Principle of Rational Discussion and explain why we are justified in adopting it when we reason with others.

3. What should you do if you find that the Principle of Rational Discussion is not applicable in a discussion you are having?

4. You find that a close friend is an alcoholic. You want to help her. You want to convince her to stop drinking. Which is more appropriate, to reason with her or take her to an Alcoholics Anonymous meeting? Explain why.

5. Since most people don't really satisfy the Principle of Rational Discussion, why not just use bad arguments to fit the circumstances?

6. You're talking to your doctor about why you're feeling ill.
    a. In analyzing what you say, should your doctor assume the Principle of Rational Discussion?

    b. In telling you what to do for your illness, should your doctor assume the Principle of Rational Discussion?

7. State the guide we have in judging when to add or delete a premise and what would count as a suitable unstated premise.

8. When can't you repair an argument?

9. Which is riskier, adding unstated premises or an unstated conclusion? Why?

10. Find (not in the text) an argument that depends on at least one unstated premise.

11. Find (not in the text) an argument that has an unstated conclusion.

12. a.   What is an indicator word?

    b.   List at least five words or phrases not in the chart that indicate a conclusion.

    c.   List at least five words or phrases not in the chart that indicate premises.

    d.   Some indicator words tell us what a speaker thinks of a claim or argument. For
         example, when the conclusion is introduced by "probably" we understand that the
         speaker thinks the argument is strong, not valid. List five more words or phrases
         that show an attitude toward a claim.

    e.   Bring in an argument from some source that uses indicator words.

13. Mark which of the blanks below would normally be filled with a premise (P) and which
    with a conclusion (C).
    a.   i_____, ii_____, iii_____, therefore, iv _____.
    b.   i_____, since, ii_____, iii_____, and, iv _____.
    c.   Because i_____, it follows that ii_____ and iii_____.
    d.   Since i_____, and ii_____, it follows that iii_____, because iv_____.
    e.   i_____ and ii_____, and that's why iii_____.
    f.   Due to i_____ and ii_____, we have iii_____.

g. In view of i_____, ii_____, and iii_____, we get iv _____.

h. From i_____ and ii_____, we can derive iii_____.

i. If i_____, then it follows that ii_____, for iii_____ and iv _____.

14. Rewrite the following argument using indicator words.

A college education will be useful to you later in life. You will probably earn more money. You'll certainly have a better chance at doing work you enjoy. You'll understand the world better, especially if you've taken a critical thinking course. And you'll be able to get a better mate. And impress your friends. And it'll make your mother happy.

15. How should we understand the charge that a premise in an argument is irrelevant?

16. a. Make up an argument against the idea that lying is a good way to convince people.

b. Convert your argument in (a) to show that reasoning badly on purpose is not effective or ethical.

17. Look at the Gettysburg Address and determine if it is an argument.

We've learned that arguments often need to be repaired. Tom's trying to apply that idea to some exercises. He's supposed to answer the italicized questions. I'll let you see what I've written about his answers.

I'm telling you I'm not at fault. How could I be? She hit me from the rear. Anytime you get rear-ended it's not your fault.

Argument? (yes or no) Yes.

Conclusion: I'm not at fault.

Premises: She hit me from the rear. Anytime you get rear-ended it's not your fault.

Additional premises needed to make it valid or strong (if none, say so): She was speeding.

Classify (with the additional premises): valid very strong ——X—— weak

Good argument? (Choose one with an explanation.)

√ It's good (passes the three tests).   with the added premise.

It's valid or strong, but you don't know if the premises are true, so you can't say if it's good or bad.

It's bad because it's unrepairable (state which of the reasons apply).

No! The argument as originally stated was valid. Why try to repair it? And if you do add a premise, then you must check either "valid or very strong"—there's no other point in adding a premise. Besides, why do you think this premise would seem plausible to the speaker? You're making up a story, not repairing this argument.

Anyone who studies hard gets good grades. So Zoe studies hard.

Argument? (yes or no) Yes.

Conclusion: Zoe must study hard.

Premises: Anyone who studies hard gets good grades.

Additional premises needed to make it valid or strong (if none, say so):
Zoe gets good grades.

Classify (with the additional premises): <u>valid</u> very strong ———— weak

Good argument? (Choose one with an explanation.)

√ It's good (passes the three tests).   with the added premise.

It's valid or strong, but you don't know if the premises are true, so you can't say if it's good or bad.

It's bad because it's unrepairable (state which of the reasons apply).

No! Zoe could get good grades and not study hard if she's very bright. It's the obvious premise to add, all right, but it makes the argument weak. The argument is unrepairable. See Example 2.

Celia must love the coat I gave her. She wears it all the time.

Argument? (yes or no) Yes.

Conclusion: Celia loves the coat I gave her.

Premises: She wears it all the time.

Additional premises needed to make it valid or strong (if none, say so): Anyone who wears a coat all the time loves it.

Classify (with the additional premises): valid very strong ——X—— weak

Good argument? (Choose one with an explanation.)

√ It's good (passes the three tests).   with the added premise.

It's valid or strong, but you don't know if the premises are true, so you can't say
    if it's good or bad.

It's bad because it's unrepairable (state which of the reasons apply).

You've confused whether an argument is valid or strong with whether it's good. With your added premise, the argument is indeed valid. But the premise you added is clearly false. Weakening it to make the argument just strong won't do—the person making the argument intended it to be valid (that "must" in the conclusion). So the argument is unrepairable because the obvious premise to add to make it valid is false.

I got sick after eating shrimp last month. Then this week again when I ate shrimp I got a rash. So I shouldn't eat shellfish anymore.

Argument? (yes or no) Yes.

Conclusion: I shouldn't eat shellfish anymore.

Premises: I got sick after eating shrimp last month. This week again when I ate shrimp
    I got a rash.

Additional premises needed to make it valid or strong (if none, say so):
    None.

Classify (with the additional premises):   valid very strong X———————— weak

Good argument? (Choose one with an explanation.)

It's good (passes the three tests).

√ It's valid or strong, but you don't know if the premises are true, so you can't say
    if it's good or bad.   Sounds very strong to me. I sure wouldn't risk eating
        shrimp again.

It's bad because it's unrepairable (state which of the reasons apply).

I agree, I wouldn't risk eating shrimp again, either. But that doesn't make the argument strong—there are lots of other possibilities for why the person got a rash. The argument is only moderate. <u>Risk may determine how strong an argument we're willing to accept, but it doesn't affect how strong the argument actually is.</u>

Our congressman voted to give more money to people on welfare. So he doesn't care about working people.

Argument? (yes or no) Yes.

Conclusion: Our congressman doesn't care about working people.

Premises: Our congressman voted to give more money to people on welfare.

Additional premises needed to make it valid or strong (if none, say so):
    I can't think of any that are plausible.

Classify (with the additional premises):   valid very strong ————————X weak

Good argument? (Choose one with an explanation.)

It's good (passes the three tests).

It's valid or strong, but you don't know if the premises are true, so you can't say
    if it's good or bad.

√ It's bad because it's unrepairable (state which of the reasons apply).

The only premise I can think of that would even make the argument strong is something like "Almost anyone who votes to give more money to people on welfare doesn't care about working people." And I know that's false. So the argument is unrepairable, right?

Right! Excellent work.

When I get near a cat, my tongue swells. I sneeze 10 times in a row, and I get a rash all over my body. I must be allergic to cats.

Argument? (yes or no) Yes.

Conclusion: I am allergic to cats.

Premises: When I get near a cat, my tongue swells.

When I get near a cat I sneeze 10 times in a row.

When I get near a cat, I get a rash all over my body.

Additional premises needed to make it valid or strong (if none, say so): Anyone whose tongue swells, sneezes 10 times in a row, and gets a rash whenever he is near a cat is allergic to cats.

Classify (with the additional premises): <u>valid</u> very strong ———————— weak

Good argument? (Choose one with an explanation.)

√ It's good (passes the three tests).   The added premise is plausible, and makes the argument valid.

It's valid or strong, but you don't know if the premises are true, so you can't say if it's good or bad.

It's bad because it's unrepairable (state which of the reasons apply).

Great! You've clearly got the idea here.   I'm sure you can do more of these now if you'll just remember that sometimes the correct answer is that the argument is unrepairable. Review those five conditions on p. 70 of the text.

Analyze the following exercises by filling in after the questions in italics.

18. George walks like a duck. George looks like a duck. George quacks like a duck. So George is a duck.

Argument? (yes or no)

Conclusion:

Premises:

Additional premises needed to make it valid or strong (if none, say so):

Classify: valid   very strong ———————— weak

Good argument? (Choose one with an explanation.)

It's good (passes the three tests).

It's valid or strong, but you don't know if the premises are true, so you can't say if it's good or bad.

It's bad because it's unrepairable (state which of the reasons apply).

19. If you're so smart, why aren't you rich?

Argument? (yes or no)

Conclusion:

Premises:

Additional premises needed to make it valid or strong (if none, say so):

Classify: valid   very strong ——————— weak

Good argument? (Choose one with an explanation.)

It's good (passes the three tests).

It's valid or strong, but you don't know if the premises are true, so you can't say if it's good or bad.

It's bad because it's unrepairable (state which of the reasons apply).

20. You caught the flu from me? Impossible! I haven't seen you for two months.

Argument? (yes or no)

Conclusion:

Premises:

Additional premises needed to make it valid or strong (if none, say so):

Classify: valid   very strong ——————— weak

Good argument? (Choose one with an explanation.)

It's good (passes the three tests).

It's valid or strong, but you don't know if the premises are true, so you can't say if it's good or bad.

It's bad because it's unrepairable (state which of the reasons apply).

21. You caught the flu from me? Impossible! You got sick first.

Argument? (yes or no)

Conclusion:

Premises:

Additional premises needed to make it valid or strong (if none, say so):

Classify: valid   very strong ——————— weak
Good argument? (Choose one with an explanation.)
    It's good (passes the three tests).
    It's valid or strong, but you don't know if the premises are true, so you can't say
       if it's good or bad.
    It's bad because it's unrepairable (state which of the reasons apply).

22. Mary Ellen just bought a Mercedes. So Mary Ellen must be rich.
    Argument? (yes or no)
    Conclusion:

    Premises:

    Additional premises needed to make it valid or strong (if none, say so):

    Classify: valid   very strong ——————— weak
    Good argument? (Choose one with an explanation.)
        It's good (passes the three tests).
        It's valid or strong, but you don't know if the premises are true, so you can't say
           if it's good or bad.
        It's bad because it's unrepairable (state which of the reasons apply).

23. All great teachers are tough graders. So Dr. E is a great teacher.
    Argument? (yes or no)
    Conclusion:

    Premises:

    Additional premises needed to make it valid or strong (if none, say so):

    Classify: valid   very strong ——————— weak
    Good argument? (Choose one with an explanation.)
        It's good (passes the three tests).
        It's valid or strong, but you don't know if the premises are true, so you can't say
           if it's good or bad.
        It's bad because it's unrepairable (state which of the reasons apply).

24. No dog meows. So Spot will only eat dry dog food.
    Argument? (yes or no)
    Conclusion:

Premises:

Additional premises needed to make it valid or strong (if none, say so):

Classify: valid very strong ——————— weak
Good argument? (Choose one with an explanation.)
    It's good (passes the three tests).
    It's valid or strong, but you don't know if the premises are true, so you can't say
        if it's good or bad.
    It's bad because it's unrepairable (state which of the reasons apply).

25. This banana is green, so it's not ripe.
    Argument? (yes or no)
    Conclusion:

Premises:

Additional premises needed to make it valid or strong (if none, say so):

Classify: valid very strong ——————— weak
Good argument? (Choose one with an explanation.)
    It's good (passes the three tests).
    It's valid or strong, but you don't know if the premises are true, so you can't say
        if it's good or bad.
    It's bad because it's unrepairable (state which of the reasons apply).

26. All green bananas are not ripe. So this banana is not ripe.
    Argument? (yes or no)
    Conclusion:

Premises:

Additional premises needed to make it valid or strong (if none, say so):

Classify: valid very strong ——————— weak
Good argument? (Choose one with an explanation.)
    It's good (passes the three tests).
    It's valid or strong, but you don't know if the premises are true, so you can't say
        if it's good or bad.
    It's bad because it's unrepairable (state which of the reasons apply).

27. All dogs that are half-wolf are great hunters. So Anubis is half-wolf.
    Argument? (yes or no)
    Conclusion:

    Premises:

    Additional premises needed to make it valid or strong (if none, say so):

    Classify: valid   very strong ——————— weak
    Good argument? (Choose one with an explanation.)
        It's good (passes the three tests).
        It's valid or strong, but you don't know if the premises are true, so you can't say
           if it's good or bad.
        It's bad because it's unrepairable (state which of the reasons apply).

28. No cat barks. So Ralph is not a cat.
    Argument? (yes or no)
    Conclusion:

    Premises:

    Additional premises needed to make it valid or strong (if none, say so):

    Classify: valid   very strong ——————— weak
    Good argument? (Choose one with an explanation.)
        It's good (passes the three tests).
        It's valid or strong, but you don't know if the premises are true, so you can't say
           if it's good or bad.
        It's bad because it's unrepairable (state which of the reasons apply).

29. You're blue-eyed. So your parents must be blue-eyed.
    Argument? (yes or no)
    Conclusion:

    Premises:

    Additional premises needed to make it valid or strong (if none, say so):

    Classify: valid   very strong ——————— weak
    Good argument? (Choose one with an explanation.)
        It's good (passes the three tests).
        It's valid or strong, but you don't know if the premises are true, so you can't say
           if it's good or bad.
        It's bad because it's unrepairable (state which of the reasons apply).

30. All professors are required to have office hours, and Dr. E is a professor.

    Argument? (yes or no)
    Conclusion:

    Premises:

    Additional premises needed to make it valid or strong (if none, say so):

    Classify: valid   very strong ——————— weak
    Good argument? (Choose one with an explanation.)
        It's good (passes the three tests).
        It's valid or strong, but you don't know if the premises are true, so you can't say
            if it's good or bad.
        It's bad because it's unrepairable (state which of the reasons apply).

31. Dick: Harry got into college because of affirmative action.
    Suzy: Gee, I didn't know that. So Harry isn't very bright.

    Argument? (yes or no)
    Conclusion:

    Premises:

    Additional premises needed to make it valid or strong (if none, say so):

    Classify: valid   very strong ——————— weak
    Good argument? (Choose one with an explanation.)
        It's good (passes the three tests).
        It's valid or strong, but you don't know if the premises are true, so you can't say
            if it's good or bad.
        It's bad because it's unrepairable (state which of the reasons apply).

32. All students who study hard are liked by their teachers. So Zoe studies hard.

    Argument? (yes or no)
    Conclusion:

    Premises:

    Additional premises needed to make it valid or strong (if none, say so):

    Classify: valid   very strong ——————— weak
    Good argument? (Choose one with an explanation.)
        It's good (passes the three tests).
        It's valid or strong, but you don't know if the premises are true, so you can't say
            if it's good or bad.
        It's bad because it's unrepairable (state which of the reasons apply).

33. They should fire Professor Zzzyzzx because he has such a bad accent that no one can understand his lectures.

Argument? (yes or no)
Conclusion:

Premises:

Additional premises needed to make it valid or strong (if none, say so):

Classify: valid   very strong ——————— weak
Good argument? (Choose one with an explanation.)
   It's good (passes the three tests).
   It's valid or strong, but you don't know if the premises are true, so you can't say
      if it's good or bad.
   It's bad because it's unrepairable (state which of the reasons apply).

34. —That masked man saved us.
    —Did you see he has silver bullets in his gunbelt?
    —And he called his horse Silver.
    —Didn't he call his friend Tonto?
    —He must be the Lone Ranger.

Argument? (yes or no)
Conclusion:

Premises:

Additional premises needed to make it valid or strong (if none, say so):

Classify: valid   very strong ——————— weak
Good argument? (Choose one with an explanation.)
   It's good (passes the three tests).
   It's valid or strong, but you don't know if the premises are true, so you can't say
      if it's good or bad.
   It's bad because it's unrepairable (state which of the reasons apply).

35. My buddies Tom, Dick, and Harry all took Dr. E's Philosophy 102 class and did well. So I should sign up for it, too. I need a good mark.

Argument? (yes or no)
Conclusion:

Premises:

Additional premises needed to make it valid or strong (if none, say so):

Classify: valid   very strong ——————— weak
Good argument? (Choose one with an explanation.)
  It's good (passes the three tests).
  It's valid or strong, but you don't know if the premises are true, so you can't say
    if it's good or bad.
  It's bad because it's unrepairable (state which of the reasons apply).

36.

Argument? (yes or no)
Conclusion:

Premises:

Additional premises needed to make it valid or strong (if none, say so):

Classify: valid   very strong ——————— weak
Good argument? (Choose one with an explanation.)
  It's good (passes the three tests).
  It's valid or strong, but you don't know if the premises are true, so you can't say
    if it's good or bad.
  It's bad because it's unrepairable (state which of the reasons apply).

37. Our college president should spend more time with the students here. Otherwise
    (s)he'd be neglecting one of the most important duties as president of the college.
    Argument? (yes or no)
    Conclusion:

Premises:

Additional premises needed to make it valid or strong (if none, say so):

Classify: valid   very strong ——————— weak
Good argument? (Choose one with an explanation.)
    It's good (passes the three tests).
    It's valid or strong, but you don't know if the premises are true, so you can't say
       if it's good or bad.
    It's bad because it's unrepairable (state which of the reasons apply).

38. These exercises are impossible. How do they expect us to get them right? There are no
right answers! They're driving me crazy.
Argument? (yes or no)
Conclusion:

Premises:

Additional premises needed to make it valid or strong (if none, say so):

Classify: valid   very strong ——————— weak
Good argument? (Choose one with an explanation.)
    It's good (passes the three tests).
    It's valid or strong, but you don't know if the premises are true, so you can't say
       if it's good or bad.
    It's bad because it's unrepairable (state which of the reasons apply).

39. These exercises are difficult but not impossible. Though there may not be a unique
right answer, there are definitely wrong answers. There are generally not unique best
ways to analyze arguments you encounter in your daily life. The best this course can
hope to do is make you think and develop your judgment through these exercises.
Argument? (yes or no)
Conclusion:

Premises:

Additional premises needed to make it valid or strong (if none, say so):

Classify: valid   very strong ——————— weak
Good argument? (Choose one with an explanation.)
    It's good (passes the three tests).
    It's valid or strong, but you don't know if the premises are true, so you can't say
       if it's good or bad.
    It's bad because it's unrepairable (state which of the reasons apply).

40. (Advertisement)

> *Top 8 Reasons Why Ketel One Vodka*
> *Should Be Your Choice*
> 1. Smoothest vodka available
> 2. Handmade in small batches
> 3. Uses the heart of the distillate
> 4. Secret family recipe started over 300 years ago
> 5. Made in traditional copper potstills
> 6. Ketel One's long tradition of fine craftsmanship has been passed from father to son for 10 generations
> 7. Made with time-tested tools and equipment just as it was in 1691
> 8. Each batch of Ketel One is tested by the master distiller personally before being approved for bottling

Argument? (yes or no)
Conclusion:

Premises:

Additional premises needed to make it valid or strong (if none, say so):

Classify: valid   very strong ——————— weak
Good argument? (Choose one with an explanation.)
   It's good (passes the three tests).
   It's valid or strong, but you don't know if the premises are true, so you can't say
      if it's good or bad.
   It's bad because it's unrepairable (state which of the reasons apply).

Exercises for Section E

1. Suzy says, "I find fat men unattractive, so I won't date you."
   a. What has Suzy implied?

   b. What can the fellow she's talking to infer?

2. Tom: Hey, your pants have rip in them.
   Lee: Yeah. A lot of my clothes need sewing. I'm hopeless at it.
   Tom: You ought to get a girlfriend.

   What claim has Tom implied?

3. Tom: Where are you from?
   Rudy: New York.
   Tom: Oh, I'm sorry.

   What has Tom implied here?

4. The following conversation is ascribed to W.C. Fields at a formal dinner party. What can we say he implied?

   W. C. Fields: Madame, you are horribly ugly.
   Lady: Your behavior is inexcusable. You're drunk.
   W. C. Fields: I may be drunk, but tomorrow I'll be sober.

5. President Clinton said, "I smoked marijuana, but I never inhaled it." What can we infer from his remarks? Be explicit in constructing the *entire* argument.

6.   Give a recent example where you inferred a claim.

7.   Give a recent example where you implied a claim.

Writing Lesson 5

Write an argument either for or against the following:

"No one should receive financial aid their first semester at this school."

Your argument should be at most one page long.
Just list the premises and the conclusion. Nothing more. Look at the instructions for Writing Lesson 3.

Check whether your instructor has chosen a *DIFFERENT TOPIC* for this assignment.

To give you a better idea of what you're expected to do, I've included Manuel's argument on a different issue.

Manuel Luis Andrade y Castillo de Pocas
Critical Thinking
Section 2
Writing Lesson 5

Issue: The chance of contracting AIDS through sexual contact can be significantly reduced by using condoms.

Definition: "AIDS" means "Acquired Immunodeficiency Syndrome"
"significantly reduced" means by more than 50%
"using condoms" means using a condom in sexual intercourse rather than having unprotected sex

Premises:

- AIDS can only be contracted by exchanging blood or semen. *A*

- In unprotected sex there is a chance of exchanging blood or semen.

- Condoms are better than 90% effective in stopping blood and semen.*

- 90% is bigger than 50%.

- AIDS has never been known to have been contracted from sharing food, using a dirty toilet seat, from touching, or from breathing in the same room with someone who has AIDS. *B*

- If you want to avoid contracting AIDS you should use a condom. *C*

Conclusion: The chance of contracting AIDS through sexual contact can be significantly reduced by using condoms.

*I'm not sure of the exact figure, but I know it's bigger than 90%.

Good. Your argument is indeed valid. But it could easily be better. You don't need "only" in A, which is what makes me uneasy in accepting that claim. And without a reference to medical literature, I'm sure not going to accept B. But you don't need it. You can delete it and your argument is just as strong.

And the last claim, C, is really irrelevant—delete it. This isn't an editorial: You're not trying to convince someone to <u>do</u> something; you're trying to convince them an objective claim is true.

Writing Lesson 6

For each of the following write the best argument you can that has as conclusion the claim below the cartoon. List only the premises and conclusion. If you believe the best argument is only weak, explain why.

Do not make up a story about the cartoon. Use what you see in the cartoon and your common knowledge.

1.

The fellow stole the purse.

2.

A. The man at the car in the parking lot is the person who ran over the bicycle.

B. The man in the car knew he ran over the bicycle and purposely didn't stop.

3.

Crows ate farmer Hong's corn.

4.

The mother is scolding her child for breaking the flower pot.

5   Is That True?

Key Words

personal experience	appeal to authority
suspend judgment	mistaking the person for the claim
arguing backwards	appeal to common practice
mistaking the person	appeal to common belief
for the argument	phony refutation

Exercises for Sections A and B.1

1. Why can't we require that every claim made in an argument be backed up?

2. What are the three attitudes we can take toward whether a claim is true?

3. Explain why in a court of law you are sworn "to tell the truth, the whole truth, and nothing but the truth," rather than just sworn to tell the truth.

4. If the conclusion of a valid argument is false, why must one of the premises be false?

5. Give an example of a rumor or gossip you heard in your personal life recently that you believed. Did you have good reason to believe it?

6. We can tell that a rumor or gossip is coming up when someone says, "Did you hear that . . .".   Give five other phrases that alert us similarly.

    a.

    b.

    c.

    d.

    e.

7. Shouldn't you trust an encyclopedia over your own experience? Explain.

8. Give at least one example of a claim that someone made this week that you knew from your own experience was false.

9. Give an example of a claim which you believed was true from memory, but really you were making a deduction from your experience.

10. When is it reasonable for us to accept a claim that disagrees with our own experience? Give an example (not in the text) of a claim that it is reasonable for you to accept even though it appears to contradict your own experience.

11. Remember the last time this class met? Answer the following about your instructor.
    a. Male _____ or Female _____
    b. Hair color _____
    c. Eye color _____
    d. Approximate height _____
    e. Approximate weight _____
    f. Was he wearing jeans? _____   Was she wearing a skirt? _____
    g. Did he/she bring a backpack to class? _____   If so, describe it.
    h. Did he/she use notes? _____

    i.   Did he/she get to class early? _____

    j.   Did he/she wear a hat? _____

    k.   Is he/she left-handed or right-handed? _____

12. Remember the last time this class met? Answer the following about the room:

    a.   How many windows? _____

    b.   How many doors? _____

    c.   How many walls? _____

    d.   Any pictures? _____

    e.   How high is the ceiling? _____

    f.   What kind of floor (concrete, tile, linoleum, carpet)? _____

    g.   How many chairs? _____

    h.   How many students showed up for class? _____

    i.   Chalkboard? _____

    j.   Lectern? _____

    k.   Faucet? _____

    l.   Wastebasket? _____

    m. Did you get out of class early? _____

13. Which of your answers to Exercises 11 and 12 were from actual memory, and which were inferences?

14. The state of the world around us can affect our observations and make our personal experience unreliable. You could honestly say you were sure the other driver didn't put on a turn signal, when it was the rain and distractions that made you not notice. List at least five ways that the *physical conditions around us* can affect our observations.

    a.

    b.

    c.

    d.

    e.

15. Recollections of our observations can be colored by tricks of our memory, but our observations can be colored at the time by our mental state, too. (For example, if you're terrified by a gun pointed at you, you might not remember the length of hair of the assailant.) List at least five ways that your *mental state* could affect your observations.

    a.

    b.

    c.

    d.

    e.

16. Our personal observations are no better than _____ ?

17. What does a bad argument tell us about its conclusion?

18. If an argument has one false premise and thirteen true premises, what attitude should we take towards its conclusion?

19. The thrust of Western culture has been: Seeing is believing. The thrust of Eastern culture has been: Believing is seeing. Explain the difference and give examples from your own experience.

Exercises for Sections B.2–B.5

1. Give an example of an argument that uses claims you know to be false, though not from personal experience. (Letters to the editor in a newspaper are a good source.)

2. a. Describe three people you encounter regularly whose word you trust and why you believe them.

   i.

   ii.

   iii.

   b. Give an example of a claim that one of them made that you shouldn't accept because the knowledge or expertise he or she has does not bear on that claim.

3. Describe two people you encounter regularly whose word you do not trust and why you do not believe them.

   i.

   ii.

4. List three *categories* of authorities you feel you can trust. State for what kind of claims those kind of authorities would be experts.

    category of authority   *kinds of claims they're experts on*

    a.

    b.

    c.

5. Give a recent example from some media source of an authority being quoted whose claims you accepted as true.

6. Give an example from some media source of an authority being quoted whose expertise does not bear on the claim being put forward, so you have no reason to accept the claim.

7. Give an example of an authority who made a claim recently that turned out to be false. Do you think it was a lie? Or did the person just not know it was false?

8. You're on a jury where two ballistics experts disagree on whether the bullet that killed the victim came from the defendant's gun.

    a. How would you decide which to believe?

    b. What consequences would there be for suspending judgment?

9.

How should he respond?

10. Give an example of an argument that uses contradictory premises. If you can't get one from listening to your friends, try the letters to the editor.

Exercises for Section B

1. Give an example of a plausible claim you've heard repeated so often you think it's true, but which you really have no reason to believe is true.

2. What three attitudes can we adopt towards whether a claim is true?

3. a. Give five criteria for accepting an unsupported claim.
      i.

      ii.

      iii.

      iv.

      v.

   b. Give three criteria for rejecting or not accepting an unsupported claim.
      i.

      ii.

      iii.

4. What is our most reliable source of information about the world?

5. What do we mean when we say that someone is arguing backwards?

6. Explain why we should apply the criteria listed in the summary in the order in which they are listed.

7. Your friend who's an avid fan tells you that the baseball game on Saturday has been cancelled. Five minutes later you hear on the radio that tickets are on sale for the game on Saturday. Whom do you believe? Why?

8. Your doctor tells you that the pain in your back can't be fixed without surgery. You go to the health-food store and the clerk tells you that they have a root extract that's been formulated especially for back pain and is likely to do you some good. Whom do you believe? Why?

9.

Comment on Tom's reasons for believing that steroids don't harm your body.

Tom's supposed to decide whether to accept, reject, or suspend judgment on the following claims, and give an explanation of what criteria he's using. I haven't made any comments, because all his answers are good. Like most people, Tom is a lot better at thinking critically about what other people say.

Suzy prefers to go out with athletes.

<u>accept</u>   reject   suspend judgment

criteria: Personal experience. She told me so.

Japanese are good at math.

accept   <u>*reject*</u>   *suspend judgment*

criteria: I know everyone thinks this is so, but it's just a stereotype isn't it? I know a couple who aren't <u>real</u> good at math, but maybe they mean "almost all"? It just seems so unlikely.

Crocodiles are found only in Asia and Africa.

accept   *reject*   <u>*suspend judgment*</u>

criteria: I think this is true. At least I seem to remember hearing it. Crocodiles are the ones in Africa and alligators in the U.S. But I'm not sure. So I guess I should suspend judgment.

Evaluate the claims in Exercises 10–29 by saying whether you accept, reject, or suspend judgment, and what criteria you are using to make that decision.

10. Smoking is bad for your health. (said by the Surgeon General)
    accept   *reject*   *suspend judgment*
    criteria:

11. Toads give you warts. (said by your mother)
    accept   *reject*   *suspend judgment*
    criteria:

12. Toads give you warts. (said by your doctor)
    accept   *reject*   *suspend judgment*
    criteria:

13. The moon rises in the west.
    accept   *reject*   *suspend judgment*
    criteria:

14. Almost all dogs bark.
    accept   *reject*   *suspend judgment*
    criteria:

15. The Pacers beat the Knicks 92–84 last night. (heard on your local news)
    accept   *reject*   *suspend judgment*
    criteria:

16. Mike Tyson is in better shape than Evander Holyfield for their title bout next week. (heard on ESPN)
    accept   reject   suspend judgment
    criteria:

17. It will take a 90% average in this course to get an A. (said by your instructor)
    accept   reject   suspend judgment
    criteria:

18. You were speeding. (said by a police officer)
    accept   reject   suspend judgment
    criteria:

19. Smoking gives you bad breath. (said to someone who smokes after a kiss)
    accept   reject   suspend judgment
    criteria:

20. Boise-Cascade has plans to log all old-growth forests in California.
    (said by a Sierra Club representative)
    accept   reject   suspend judgment
    criteria:

21. I still don't get it. Our instructor said that the argument in Exercise 47 was valid.
    I guess I'll just have to believe it.
    accept   reject   suspend judgment
    criteria:

22. The United States government was not involved in the recent attempt to invade Cuba.
    (unnamed sources in the Defense Department, quoted in an Associated Press story)
    accept   reject   suspend judgment
    criteria:

23. Cadillac is the best-selling luxury car in California. (in an advertisement)
    accept   reject   suspend judgment
    criteria:

24. Cadillac is the best-selling luxury car in California. (in *Consumer Reports*)
    accept   reject   suspend judgment
    criteria:

25. Cats are the greatest threat to public health of any common pets.
    (said by the author of this book)
    accept   reject   suspend judgment
    criteria:

26. Cats are the greatest threat to public health of any common pets.
    (said by the Surgeon General)
    accept   reject   suspend judgment
    criteria:

27. Cats are the greatest threat to public health of any common pets.
    (said by the Pope)
    accept   reject   suspend judgment
    criteria:

28. You left the water running when you left home today.
    (said by someone who lives with you)
    accept   reject   suspend judgment
    criteria:

29. The Big Bang with which the universe began was the work of God.
    (said by a noted astronomer)
    accept   reject   suspend judgment
    criteria:

30. Look at the front page of your local newspaper and the first page of the local section and see if you can determine who wrote each article. Can you do the same with your local TV newscast?

31. Pick a magazine you often read and tell the class what biases you expect from it. That is, what kinds of claims in it should you suspend judgment on rather than accept?

32. Which section of your local newspaper do you think is most reliable? Why?

33. a.   What part of the national newscast do you think is most likely to be true?

    b.   Which part do you think is least reliable?

34. Give an example of a news story you heard or read that you knew was biased because it didn't give the whole story.

35. What difference is there between how we evaluate an advertisement and how we evaluate any other (implicit) argument?

36. Find an advertisement and evaluate the claims in it.

37. Here are two articles. At the end of the chapter I'll tell you where they're from. Which, if either, of these do you find believable? Cite the criteria you're using.

a. **Half-Man Half-Dog Baffles Scientists**

Half-man, half-dog Kent Morley has baffled scientists who say that he has the genetic makeup of both man and canine in spite of the fact that his mother and father were human–and normal in every way!

That's the word from geneticist William Cramer, who says that the 38-year-old Morley is currently being studied at Minnesota's famed Mayo Clinic, where doctors are trying to figure out just what he is–and why Mother Nature made him that way.

"This is one of the most intriguing medical mysteries of all time," declared Dr. Cramer, who is widely considered to be one of the world's top authorities on genetic abnormalities and mutations.

"Mr. Morley has the head of a dog, the body and brain of a human being, and the behavioral characteristics of both species. Some people might be inclined to dismiss him as an ordinary freak of nature," he continued, "but nothing could be further from the truth.

"Ma Nature might make mistakes, but she doesn't make mistakes like this. Mr. Morley turned out the way he did for a reason. And some of the best minds in the field are bound and determined to find out what that reason is."

Spokesmen for the Mayo Clinic declined to comment on Dr. Cramer's report.

But the Washington-based geneticist not only stands by his story, he says clinic staffers have consulted him almost daily since the half-man, half-dog was admitted for testing and evaluation under an assumed name on March 14.

He added that Morley, who was born in Florida and now earns a very good living as a computer programmer, is extremely intelligent–with an IQ in the range of 125.

"Judging from the many tests that have been conducted to date, his brain would appear to be predominantly human," said Dr. Cramer.

"On the other hand, he exhibits some canine behavior, including a powerful hunting instinct.

"Like most dogs, he is wary of strangers. But once he gets to know you, he is extremely friendly and loyal. He also offers something that most dog owners prize in their pets–unconditional love."

Morley has been unavailable for comment. But interviews that appeared in science and medical journals over the past few years indicate that he suffered emotionally for most of his life. As a child, he was shunned by "normal" children and forced to endure the stares and comments of complete strangers who considered him to be a freak. He reportedly found both comfort and anonymity in his study of computers and related technologies.

And in recent years, he seems to have come to terms with his appearance and learned to accept himself for what he is.

In fact, Dr. Cramer says Morley met and married a 28-year-old woman who "loves his looks," late last year. And while the couple would like nothing more than to have children, they want assurances that their babies will be 100 percent human.

"It appears that Mr. Morley can father normal children but we can't be sure until the results of a few more tests are in and analyzed," Dr. Cramer said.

[There are pictures of Mr. Morley and Dr. Cramer.]

b. **Two-headed calf born in Minersville**

It would have made a great side show for a circus. The heifers at Gillins dairy in Minersville, Utah were averaging about a calf a day recently, but Monday dairy owner Wayne Gillins witnessed something he has not seen in his 50 years of dairy farming.

One of the heifers was ready to calf when, Gillins said, he and his son began to help the cow. They reached inside and could feel two hind legs. They began to try and pull the cow out, but as they got further along in aiding the birth, they found something else.

"We reached up there and could feel two tails," Gillins said. He thought for sure the heifer was having twins. They continued to try to birth the calf, but the back was too big. It became apparent they would have to take the animal to the veterinarian for a caesarean section delivery.

After some prodding with a pitch fork, Gillins and his son loaded the cow into a trailer and took it to Dr. H. Nielsen in Delta, Utah, 80 miles away. Nielsen began the operation to deliver the calf, but it was not what he had expected.

"He said to me I've got a head . . . and another head," Gillins said. But, surprise, the heifer was not delivering twins. When it was removed, the new calf had two heads, two tails, six legs and two spinal cords. It looked like a single animal with one body. The calf was the width of two newborn calves and died shortly before it was delivered. The calf had two back legs and two legs in front that appeared to be normal size for a new-born calf. Two more underdeveloped legs were on the inside between the necks of the calf.

Gillins said the calf was an embryo transplant, but he said that should not have had anything to do with the abnormal birth, because many of his calves come from such transplants and arrive with no birth defects.

The heifer had to be cut a longer length than usual to deliver the calf. Tuesday afternoon, the animal had a paralyzed right front leg. Nielsen said he was unsure what caused the paralysis.

"It's kind of different, isn't it?" Gillins said, pointing at the calf. "I've been in this business for 50 years, and I've never seen anything like this."

Nielsen said he was planning to dissect the calf Tuesday to see if the internal organs were separate as well. He said he assumed it had two hearts and other vital organs because of the structure, but he could not tell for sure without opening it up.

Nielsen said he has been practicing veterinary medicine for more than 20 years and he has seen only one other birth like this one.

He said a Scipio, Utah, beef cow gave birth to a two-headed calf with eight legs. It also died shortly after birth. While he had seen this type of birth before, Nielsen said it is still not an everyday occurrence.

"It's not real common, but it's not real uncommon, either," he said. Nielsen said if he had to guess, he would say that about one in every 100,000 births are like this one.

"It is clear that the tissue did not separate completely, but there is no indication what caused it." Nielsen said he has talked to other veterinarians who have witnessed these types of births and most of them concur that the calf dies after a few hours if it lives through the birthing process.

"They are not survivors," he said. "Even if they do survive the birth they don't live long." [There is a picture of the calf.]

Criteria used to evaluate the extracts:

38. The following was in the advertising section of a magazine. It wasn't clear if it was a paid ad or an article. Evaluate the claims by the criteria of this chapter.

Sam Louie, Pet Psychic

"Animals and people share a commonality of soul and spirit. We all search for love and we all seek to connect."

Using the same tools that many other psychics use–clairvoyance, feelings, and intuition received through the seventh chakra–Sam Louie communicates with animals. A practicing psychic since 1987, Louie found that he was increasingly "picking up" on animals and two years ago decided to focus on bridging the gap between pets and their humans.

Louie consults with pets and owners, usually via the telephone. "When someone calls, I ask for a description of the animal (color, weight, age, breed) then I focus in and contact the animal. I ask permission to communicate, tell them who I am, and then ask them if they want to talk."

People generally call with specific questions regarding their pets' behavior or health. He works with several clients who race horses, helping them to understand the animal's anxieties and needs. Many people call for a consultation when their pet is dying, asking Louie to express to the animal their love and gratitude and hoping for a final "word" from a beloved companion.

In addition to his consultations, Louie also conducts workshops in basic, intermediate and advanced animal communication. "I encourage people to develop their Buddha nature, to understand that there is no separation between souls, that we can all understand each other." Using guided meditations, imaging and other techniques, Louie teaches animal lovers to visualize communication, then helps them to re-open their innate psychic abilities and to recognize true communication when it occurs. He describes the process this way: "You have to bring forth creative imagination coupled with belief in reality."   *Catalyst,* May, 1996

39. Discuss the following advertisement in terms of the criteria given in this chapter.

$250,000

is what you can make per year playing

CRAPS

Finally: a two-part video and book written by a top Las
Vegas gaming expert that is easy to follow. In fact it's

CRAP$ MADE EASY

You do not need a large bankroll to get started.

Order toll free 1-800-xxx-xxxx and receive

- 1 hour instructional video
- 150 page book with graphs charts, and inside tips,
- Pocket-sized game card for quick reference
- Felt layout for home play
- Regulation dice and playing chips

... $59.95 . . .

40. Find an article that has quotes from some "think-tank" or "institute." Find out what
bias that group would have.

Exercises for Sections C

1. a. What is an appeal to authority?

   b. Is every appeal to authority bad? Explanation or example.

2. Why should you never mistake the person for the argument?

3. When are we justified in rejecting a claim because of who said it?

4. a. What is an appeal to common belief?

   b. How does it differ from an appeal to common practice?

   c. Give an example of either an appeal to common belief or practice that you heard this last week.

5. What do we call it when someone gives too much deference to an authority?

6. Hypocrisy is bad. So why shouldn't we reject anything that smacks of hypocrisy?

7. What does it mean to say that a person has made a phony refutation?

Here are some more of Tom's exercises. He's trying to see if he can distinguish between good and bad reasons for accepting or rejecting claims. I'm including my comments.

> **Doctor Ball said that for me to lose weight I need to get more exercise, but he's so obese. So I'm not going to listen to him.**
>
> This person is mistaking the person for the claim. Looks like a phony refutation to me.
>
> *That's right.*

> **Lucy said I shouldn't go see Doctor Williams because he's had problems with malpractice suits in the past. But Lucy also believes in herbs and natural healing, so she's not going to like any doctors.**
>
> Looks O.K. to me. The speaker is just questioning the authority of Lucy and deciding not to accept her claim.
>
> *No. It's a case of mistaking the person for the argument. The speaker isn't suspending judgment on a claim, but is rejecting Suzy's argument.*

> **Zoe: Everyone should exercise. It's good for you. It keeps you in shape, gives you more energy, and keeps away depression.**
>
> **Dick: Are you kidding? I've never seen you exercise.**
>
> Phony refutation.
>
> *Right!*

For Exercises 8–20 answer:

a. Does it fit into one or more of the classifications of this section?

b. Is it a bad argument?

8. Suzy: I played doubles on my team for four years. It is definitely a more intense game than playing singles.

   Zoe: Yesterday on the news Michael Chang said that doubles in tennis is much easier because there are two people covering almost the same playing area.

   Suzy: I guess he must be right then.

9. Mom: You shouldn't stay out so late. It's dangerous, so I want you home early.

   Son: But none of my friends have curfews and they stay out as long as they want.

10. Manuel: Barbara said divorce'll hurt her kids' emotions.

    Maria: But she goes out with her boyfriend every night leaving the kids and her husband at home. She doesn't divorce, but she's already hurt her kids. So it doesn't matter if she gets divorced or not.

11. I can't solve this math question. It's too hard for a high school student. But my math teacher says the answer is 3. So the answer must be 3.

12. The Surgeon General said that smoking is bad for your health, so you should give up smoking.

13. The Surgeon General said that marijuana should not be legal, so I'm going to write my congresswoman and urge her not to support the bill legalizing marijuana.

14. Zoe: You should be more sensitive to the comments you make around people.
    Dick: Of course you'd think that, 'cause you're a woman.

15. Zoe: The author of this book said that bad people always make wrong decisions. You need to have virtue to make good use of critical thinking.
    Suzy: What does he know about virtue?

16. Suzy: Why don't you try to straighten out the problem with Dick?
    Zoe: Everyone knows it's best to let a sleeping dog lie.

17. Zoe: That program to build a new homeless shelter is a great idea.
    Suzy: How could you say that? You don't even give money to the homeless who beg on street corners.

18.

19. Tom: What do you think about requiring kids at school to wear uniforms?
    Lee: It must be good because my mother said so.

20. —We should tax cigarettes much more heavily.

    —I can't believe you said that. Don't you smoke three packs a day?

In the Exercise for Section B, Exercise 37:
   a. Was by Nick Mann/ Special Correspondent, *Weekly World News,* April 20, 1993.
   b. Was by Tyson Hiatt, *The Spectrum,* St. George, Utah, July 17, 1996.

Writing Lesson 7

Write an argument either for or against the following:

"No spacecraft landed on Mars in 1997; the photos were faked."

Your argument should be at most one page long.

Just list the premises and the conclusion in the format of the sample arguments. Nothing more.

Check whether your instructor has chosen a *DIFFERENT TOPIC* for this assignment.

You know whether you believe this claim. But why do you believe it or doubt it? Make your argument based on the criteria we studied in Chapter 5.

But what if you're unsure? You write pro and con lists, yet you can't make up your mind. You're really in doubt.

Then write the best argument you can for why someone should suspend judgment on the claim. That's not a cop-out; sometimes suspending judgment is the most mature, reasonable attitude to take. But you should have good reasons for suspending judgment, based on conflicts in the criteria of Chapter 5.

To give you a better idea of what you're expected to do, I've included arguments by Tom and Suzy on different topics.

Tom Wyzyczy
Critical Thinking
Section 4
Writing Lesson 7

Issue: Elvis is still alive.

Definition: By "Elvis" I understand Elvis Presley.
Premises:

Elvis Presley was reported to have died a number of years ago.

All the reputable press agencies reported his death.

Many people went to his funeral,^{A} which was broadcast live.^{B}

His doctor signed his death certificate, according to news reports.

There have been reports that Elvis is alive.

No such report has been in the mainstream media, only in tabloids.

No physical evidence that he is alive has ever been produced.

No one would have anything to gain by faking his death. ^{C}

If Elvis were alive, he would have much to gain by making that known
    to the public.

Conclusion: Elvis is not alive.

Good. But it could be better. First, split the third premise into two (A and B). I don't know if it was broadcast live, yet I can accept part A.

Second, the phrase "mainstream media" and "tabloid" are too vague. You should cite real sources if you want someone to accept your argument.

And premise C is very dubious: Any of his heirs had lots to gain.

Finally, you take for granted that the reader knows why some of your premises are important. But it isn't obvious. Why is A important? To explain, you need to add the glue, a premise or premises linking it to the conclusion. You're still leaving too much unstated. Don't rely too much on the other person making your argument for you. Review Chapters 3 and 4.

Still, I think you have the idea from Chapter 5 and won't be suckered by the conspiracy theorists.

Suzy Queue
Critical Thinking
Section 2
Writing Lesson 7

Issue: The CIA started the cocaine epidemic in the ghettos in order to
control and pacify blacks.

Premises:

The CIA has lied to us a lot in the past.

Riots in the past in the ghettos have been a serious problem in the U.S.

The government wants to control blacks, so they won't make any trouble.

Black people in the ghetto had too much to ~~loose~~ *lose* to start.

Many people in the ghettos believe that the CIA introduced cocaine to the U.S.

It was reported on national news that the CIA was involved with drug running
from Latin America.

Conclusion: The CIA started the cocaine epidemic in the ghettos in order to
control and pacify blacks.

At best you've given reason to <u>suspend judgment</u>. You haven't given me any reason to believe the claim is <u>true</u>, only that it isn't obviously false.

Some of your premises are way too vague ("national news," "serious problems"). And I can't see how they link to the conclusion. Are you suggesting that if the CIA lied to us in the past that makes it highly probable that they introduced cocaine into the ghettos? That's pretty weak. And big deal that a lot of people in the ghettos believe the CIA introduced cocaine there. A lot of people think the moon doesn't rise or that it rises in the west—that doesn't make it true. Are they authorities?

Review the criteria in Chapter 5.

Review Exercises for Chapters 1–5

1. What is an argument?

2. What is a claim?

3. a. What is an objective claim?

   b. Give an example of an objective claim.

   c. Give an example of a subjective claim.

4. What does it mean to say a sentence is ambiguous?

5. Can a vague sentence be a claim? Explain.

6. Is a definition a claim? Explain.

7. a. What is a persuasive definition?

   b. Give an example.

8. What is the definition of a "good argument"?

9.   What three tests must an argument pass for it to be good?

10. a.   What is a valid argument?

    b.   Give an example of a valid argument that is good.

    c.   Give an example of a valid argument that is bad.

11. a.   What does it mean to say an argument is strong?

    b.   Give an example of a strong argument that is good.

    c.   Give an example of a strong argument that is bad.

12. Is every weak argument bad? Explain.

13. How do you show an argument is not valid?

14. If an argument has fourteen true premises and one false premise, should we accept the the conclusion? Explain.

15. If an argument is bad, what does that tell us about its conclusion?

16. Is every valid or strong argument with true premises good? Explain.

17. Should we always prefer valid arguments to strong arguments? Explain.

18. What is the main mark of irrationality?

19. State the Principle of Rational Discussion.

20. State the Guide to Repairing Arguments.

21. Give five circumstances in which we shouldn't repair an argument.

22. a. What is an indicator word?

    b. Is an indicator word part of a claim?

23. What is our most reliable source of information about the world?

24. What three attitudes can we take toward whether a claim is true?

25. Give five criteria for accepting an unsupported claim.

26. Give three criteria for rejecting or not accepting an unsupported claim.

27. What does it mean to say that someone is arguing backwards?

28. What does it mean to say someone is mistaking the person for the argument?

29. When are we justified in rejecting a claim because someone said it?

30. When are we justified in rejecting an argument because someone said it?

31. What is a phony refutation?

6 Compound Claims

Key Words

compound claim	direct way
"or" claim	of reasoning with conditionals
alternative	indirect way
conditional	of reasoning with conditionals
antecedent	affirming the consequent
consequent	denying the antecedent
contradictory of a claim	contrapositive
excluding possibilities	only if
inclusive "or"	sufficient condition
exclusive "or"	necessary condition
false dilemma	reasoning in a chain with conditionals
	slippery slope argument

Exercises for Section A

1. What is a compound claim?

2. Why can we take both A and B to be premises when someone says "A and B"?

3. a. What is a conditional?

   b. Is a conditional a compound claim?

4. Make a conditional promise to your instructor you believe you can keep.

5. What do we call the parts of an "or" claim?

For each of Exercises 6–9, if it is an "or" claim, identify the alternatives.

6. Either Dick loves Zoe best, or he loves Spot best.

7. You're either for me or against me.

8. You'd better stop smoking in here or else!

9. AIDS cannot be contracted by touching nor by breathing air in the same room as a person infected with AIDS.

10. What is the antecedent of a conditional?

11. Give five examples (not from the text) of conditional claims that don't use the word "if" or don't use the word "then." At least one should have the consequent first and antecedent last. Exchange with a classmate to identify the antecedents and consequents.

12. What is the contradictory of a claim?

13. How do you say the contradictory of "A or B"?

14. How do you say the contradictory of "If A then B"?

15. Write the contradictory of:

  a.   Inflation will go up or interest rates will go up.

  b.   Maria or Manuel will pick up Dick at the airport.

  c.   Zoe will serve either mustard greens or brussels sprouts at dinner.

  d.   Manuel won't take the exam on Tuesday.

  e.   Maria will go shopping and Manuel will cook.

  f.   If Maria goes shopping, then Manuel will cook.

16. Make up two conditionals and two "or" claims. Exchange them with a classmate to write the contradictories.

Here are two examples of Tom's work on conditionals.

Getting an A in critical thinking means that you studied hard.
Conditional? (yes or no) Yes.
Antecedent: You get an A in critical thinking.
Consequent: You studied hard.
Contradictory: You got an A in critical thinking but you didn't study hard.
      (or Even though you got an A in critical thinking, you didn't study hard.)
Good work.

Spot loves Dick because Dick plays with him.
Conditional? (yes or no) No.
Antecedent: Spot loves Dick. *No*
Consequent: Dick plays with him. *No*

Contradictory: Spot loves Dick but Dick doesn't play with him. *No*

> *You're right, it's not a conditional: the word "because" tells you it's an argument. But if it's not a conditional, then there is no antecedent and no consequent. And there can't be a contradictory of an argument.*

For Exercises 17–28 fill in after the italics.

17. If the Israelis and Palestinians agree on the next step of the peace process, then Syria will make peace with Israel.
    Conditional? (yes or no)
    Antecedent:
    Consequent:
    Contradictory:

18. If you don't apologize I'll never talk to you again.
    Conditional? (yes or no)
    Antecedent:
    Consequent:
    Contradictory:

19. Neither Maria nor Manuel will travel at Christmas.
    Conditional? (yes or no)
    Antecedent:
    Consequent:
    Contradictory:

20. Loving someone means you never throw dishes at them.
    Conditional? (yes or no)
    Antecedent:
    Consequent:
    Contradictory:

21. Lee never writes to his brother.
    Conditional? (yes or no)
    Antecedent:
    Consequent:
    Contradictory:

22. Since 2 times 2 is 4, and 4 times 2 is 8, I should be ahead $8, not $7.
    Conditional? (yes or no)
    Antecedent:
    Consequent:
    Contradictory:

23. Spot is a good dog, even though he attacked your cat.
    Conditional? (yes or no)
    Antecedent:
    Consequent:
    Contradictory:

24. "If Spot attacked your cat, then I'll pay for the funeral," said Dick.
    Conditional? (yes or no)
    Antecedent:
    Consequent:
    Contradictory:

25. Dick or Zoe will go to the grocery to get eggs.
    Conditional? (yes or no)
    Antecedent:
    Consequent:
    Contradictory:

26. If it's really true that if Dick takes Spot for a walk he'll do the dishes, then Dick won't take Spot for a walk.
    Conditional? (yes or no)
    Antecedent:
    Consequent:
    Contradictory:

27. If Dick goes to the basketball game, then he either got a free ticket or he borrowed money for one.
    Conditional? (yes or no)
    Antecedent:
    Consequent:
    Contradictory:

28. Dick will love Zoe so long as she treats Spot well.
    Conditional? (yes or no)
    Antecedent:
    Consequent:
    Contradictory:

Exercises for Section B

1. Give an "or" claim that you know is true, though you don't know which of the alternatives is true.

2. State the form of valid arguments that use "or" claims.

3. What is a false dilemma?

4. Give an example of a false dilemma you've used or had used on you recently.

5. Why is using a false dilemma so good at making people do what you want them to do? Is it a good way to convince?

6. Sometimes a false dilemma is stated using "if . . . then . . .":

   If you don't stop smoking, you're going to die.
      (Either you stop smoking or you will die.)

   Mommy, if you don't take me to the circus, then you don't really love me.
      (Either you take me to the circus or you don't love me.)

   If you can't remember what you wanted to say, it's not important.
      (Either you remember what you want to say or it's not important.)

   Give two examples of false dilemmas stated using "if . . . then . . ." Give them to a classmate to rewrite as "or" claims.

7. A particular form of false dilemma is the *perfectionist dilemma,* which assumes:

> Either the situation will be perfect if we do this, or we shouldn't do it.
> (*All or nothing at all.*)

For example,

— I'm voting for raising property taxes to pay for improvements to the schools.
— Don't be a fool. No matter how much money they pour into the schools, they'll never be first rate.

Give an example of a perfectionist dilemma you've heard or read.

8. a. Give two examples of "or" claims that are best understood as meaning that the alternatives exclude each other (*exclusive* "or").

   b. An argument that relies on a dubious claim that says it has to be one or the other but not both is a *false exclusive dilemma.* Give an example.

Evaluate Exercises 9–13 by filling in after the italics.

9. Either Suzy loves Tom or she's putting on a good show. But she's a lousy actress. So she must really love Tom.
   Argument? (yes or no)
   Conclusion (if unstated, add it):

   Premises:

   Additional premises needed (if none, say so):

   Classify (with the additional premises): valid   very strong ——————— weak
   Good argument? (yes or no, with an explanation) (If it's a false dilemma, say so.)

10. Dick : It's time. Either we get married or we should stop living together.
    Zoe: What do you mean "It's time"?
    Dick: I mean we both know that just living together is awkward.
    Zoe: Well, I don't want to live alone. Do you?
    Dick: No. So we'll have to get married.
    (Evaluate the whole dialogue as one argument.)
    Argument? (yes or no)
    Conclusion (if unstated, add it):

    Premises:

    Additional premises needed (if none, say so):

    Classify (with the additional premises):   valid   very strong —————— weak
    Good argument? (yes or no, with an explanation) (If it's a false dilemma, say so.)

11. Zoe: We should get rid of Spot. He keeps chewing on everything in the house.
    Dick: But why does that mean we should get rid of him?
    Zoe: Because either we train him to stop chewing or get rid of him. And we
           haven't been able to train him.
    Dick: But I love Spot. We can just make him live outdoors.
    (Evaluate what Zoe says as an argument. Consider Dick's answer in doing so.)
    Argument? (yes or no)
    Conclusion (if unstated, add it):

    Premises:

    Additional premises needed (if none, say so):

    Classify (with the additional premises):   valid   very strong —————— weak
    Good argument? (yes or no, with an explanation) (If it's a false dilemma, say so.)

12. Zoe: Either you do the dishes and take out the trash or I'm leaving you.
    Dick: Hey, I'm a man, that's not man's work.
    Zoe: Then I'm leaving you.

Argument? (yes or no)
Conclusion (if unstated, add it):

Premises:

Additional premises needed (if none, say so):

Classify (with the additional premises):   valid   very strong ——————— weak
Good argument? (yes or no, with an explanation) (If it's a false dilemma, say so.)

13. I'm not going to vote, because no matter who is president I still won't get a job.
Argument? (yes or no)
Conclusion (if unstated, add it):

Premises:

Additional premises needed (if none, say so):

Classify (with the additional premises):   valid   very strong ——————— weak
Good argument? (yes or no, with an explanation) (If it's a false dilemma, say so.)

Exercises for Section C.1

If Dick and Jane get
another dog,

If Dick spends more
time with Spot,

Then Spot will
be happy!

If Dick buys Spot a
juicy new bone,

If Spot finally learns how
to catch field mice,

1. Assume all the conditionals represented in the picture are true. Using them:

    a. Give two examples of the Direct Way of reasoning.

    b. Give two examples of the Indirect Way of reasoning.

    c. Give two examples of Affirming the Consequent. Explain why each is not valid
        in terms of other possibilities.

    d. Give two examples of Denying the Antecedent. Explain why each is not valid in terms of other possibilities.

2. Give an example (not from the text) of the Direct Way of reasoning with conditionals.

3. Give an example (not from the text) of the Indirect Way of reasoning with conditionals.

4. Give an example (not from the text) of Affirming the Consequent. Show it's not valid.

5. Give an example (not from the text) of Denying the Antecedent. Show it's not valid.

6. State the contrapositive of:
    a. If Flo plays with Spot, then she has to take a bath.

    b. If Manuel doesn't get his wheelchair fixed by Wednesday, he can't attend class on Thursday.

    c. If Maria goes with Manuel to the dance, then Lee will be home alone on Saturday.

For Exercises 7–12, if there's a claim you can add to make the argument valid according to one of the forms we studied, add it. If the argument is unrepairable, say so.

7. If Flo comes over early to play, then Spot will bark. So Spot barked.

8.   Whenever Flo comes over to play, Spot barks. So Flo didn't come over to play.

9.   Tom: Zoe will cook spaghetti if Dick remembered to buy tomato paste.
     Harry: So it's definitely spaghetti tonight.

10. Zoe will wash the dishes if Dick cooks. So Dick didn't cook.

11. Lee: Dr. E gives multiple choice exams when he has no time to grade regular exams.
     Suzy: So Dr. E won't give a multiple choice exam today.

12. If Flo does her homework, then she can watch TV. So Flo did her homework.

13. Here's another valid form of reasoning with conditionals:

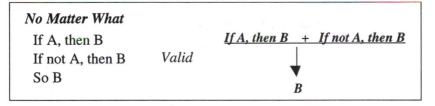

Dick: If I study for my math exam this weekend we won't be able to have a good
       time at the beach.
Zoe: But if you don't study for your exam, you'll worry about it like you always
       do, and we won't be able to have a good time at the beach. So it looks like
       this weekend is shot.

Give another example of this form.

Exercises for Sections C.2 and C.3

1. We know that the following are equivalent:

    > Dick will go to the movies only if he gets home before 6 p.m.
    > If Dick didn't get home before 6 p.m., then he didn't go to the movies.
    > If Dick went to the movies, then he got home before 6 p.m.

    Rewrite each of the following in two ways:

    a. You can pass this course only if you study hard.

    b. I'll love you only if you love me.

    c. You can get AIDS only if you're stupid or unlucky.

2. a. Give two examples (not from the text) of "only if" claims that you know are true.

    b. Rewrite them in the form "if A, then B."

    c. Rewrite them in the form "if not B, then not A."

For Exercises 3–10 state which of the following hold:

   (i) is necessary for (ii)   (i) is both necessary and sufficient for (ii)
   (i) is sufficient for (ii)   (i) is neither necessary nor sufficient for (ii)

3. (i) The ground outdoors is wet.   (ii) It's raining hard.

4. (i) The Packers scored a touchdown.   (ii) The Packers are winning.

5. (i) Zoe won $47 at blackjack.   (ii) Zoe was gambling.

6. (i) Suzy is lying.   (ii) Suzy isn't telling the truth.

7. (i) Maria has a restraining order on her ex-husband.
   (ii) Maria's ex-husband is prohibited by law from approaching her.

8. (i) Ralph is a dog.   (ii) Ralph chases cats.

9. (i) Suzy is over 21.   (ii) Suzy can legally drink in this state.

10. (i) Tom was charged with DUI.   (ii) Tom was found guilty of DUI.

Often we say that one condition is necesary or sufficient for another, like "Being over 16 is necessary for getting a driver's license." That means that the general conditional is true: "If you can get a driver's license, then you're over 16." For Exercises 11–15 state which condition is necessary or sufficient, as for Exercises 3–10.

11. (i) being a dog   (ii) being an animal

12. (i) being a U.S. citizen   (ii) being born in the U.S.

13. (i) being a U.S. citizen   (ii) being allowed to vote in the U.S.

14. (i) having the ability to fly   (ii) being a bird

15. (i) being a sister   (ii) being a female

16. What is a necessary condition for there to be a fire?

17. What is a necessary condition for being a father?

18. What is a sufficient condition for passing this course?

19. What is a necessary condition for performing open heart surgery?

For each of Exercises 20–28, rewrite it as an "if . . . then . . ." claim if that is possible. If it's not, say so.

20. Flo will go over to play with Spot only if her mother lets her.

21. Eating nutritious dog food is necessary for Spot to be healthy.

22. Paying the garbageman $5 is necessary for Dick to sleep late.

23. Only if Zoe's mother doesn't come for the holidays will Dick and Zoe go to Mexico.

24. Suzy will get an A in critical thinking only if Dr. E is drunk when he fills out grades.

25. Suzy will get an A in critical thinking if Dr. E reads his grade sheet wrong and confuses her with Maria, who's next on the list.

26. Tom loves Suzy even though she hasn't a clue in the critical thinking class.

27. Of course, Suzy loves Tom despite the coach suspending him for a game.

28. For Tom to get back on the team, he has to do 200 push-ups.

29. Give an example in which someone has argued for a condition being necessary, when what he or she should be arguing for is that it is sufficient.

30. A *if and only if* B   means   if A then B, and if B then A

    For example, suppose Dick is such a heavy sleeper that the only way he will wake up is if Spot barks. Then there's only one route to "Dick will wake up." We have both:

    > If Spot barks, then Dick will wake up.
    > If Dick wakes up, then Spot barked.

    So we can say:

    > Spot will bark *if and only if* Dick wakes up.

    Give an example of an "if and only if" claim from your own life that you know is true.

Exercises for Chapter 6

1. Make a list of the valid argument forms we studied in this chapter.

2. Make a list of the invalid argument forms we studied in this chapter.

3. Make a list of the bad argument types we studied in this chapter.

4. What does it mean to say someone is reasoning in a chain with conditionals?

5. What's a slippery slope argument?

6. Rewrite the credit card argument in Section C.4 to show that it is reasoning in a chain.

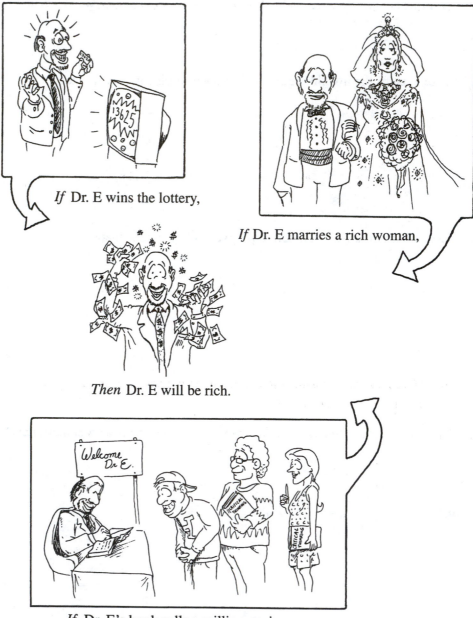

If Dr. E wins the lottery,

If Dr. E marries a rich woman,

Then Dr. E will be rich.

If Dr. E's book sells a million copies,

7. Assume that all the conditionals represented in the picture are true.

a.   State all the true "only if" claims from the picture.

b.   Rewrite each "if. . .then . . ." claim as its contrapositive.

c.   Write the contradictory of each "if . . . then . . ." claim.

d.   Give an example using the claims in the picture of each of the valid and invalid forms using conditionals.

    e.   Give an example using the claims in the picture of each of the valid and invalid forms except that in each you use an "only if" claim.

    f.   State which claims are sufficient for which others.

    h.   State which claims are necessary for which others.

    i.   Explain why you enjoyed this exercise so much. Do not use any four-letter words.

8. Make up flash cards to learn how to recognize the forms of arguments we studied in this chapter. On the back of a card, put the form (for example, If A then B, not A, so not B). Write whether it's valid or invalid. On the front put an example you've made up. Make three cards for each form, each card showing a different example. Some of the examples should have a conditional that isn't already in "if . . . then . . ." form. Practice with your own cards. Trade with a fellow student. If you're not sure that your examples illustrate the forms, ask your instructor.

Here are more of Tom's homeworks with my comments. He's supposed to evaluate the argument, noting whether it uses a particular valid or invalid or bad argument form.

Suzy: If you apologize to Zoe, I'm sure she'll help you go look for Spot.

Dick: It's her fault he got loose. I won't apologize.

Suzy: Then she won't help you look for Spot.

Argument? (the whole dialogue) (yes or no) Yes.

Conclusion (if unstated, add it): Zoe won't help Dick look for Spot.

Premises: If you apologize to Zoe, she'll help you go look for Spot. It's Zoe's fault Spot got loose. Dick won't apologize to Zoe.

Additional premises needed (if none, say so): None.

Classify (with the additional premises): Valid.

Good argument? (yes or no, with an explanation) Good. It's the direct way of reasoning with conditionals.

> *No. It's a case of denying the antecedent. The premises are true, all right, but Zoe did go help Dick. She felt guilty.*

Zoe: I'll go hiking with you only if you'll go to this movie with me.

Dick: O.K., I'll go to the movie.

(A week later, after Dick's gone to a Jane Austen movie with Zoe)

Zoe: I'm not going to go hiking with you. You ruined my dinner party.

Did Zoe go back on her word? Yes. It's the direct way of reasoning with conditionals. Zoe made a conditional promise and didn't follow through.

> *No. Zoe said she's go <u>only if</u> Dick went to the movie, not <u>if</u> he went to the movie. Review <u>only if</u> vs <u>if</u>.*

If you don't give to charity you're selfish. If you pay all your bills on time with nothing left over, you can't give to charity. Since you don't want to be selfish, you shouldn't pay all your bills on time.

Argument? (yes or no) Yes.

Conclusion (if unstated, add it): You shouldn't pay all your bills on time.

Premises: If you don't give to charity you're selfish. If you pay all your bills on time with nothing left over, you can't give to charity. You don't want to be selfish.

Additional premises needed (if none, say so): When you pay your bills, you have nothing left over.

Classify (with the additional premises): Valid. Reasoning in a Chain and Indirect Way.

Good argument? (yes or no, with an explanation) It looks O.K., if the premises apply to the person, but something seems wrong.

> *Good work. You recognized the form, and you're getting good at spotting what unstated premises are needed. What's wrong here is that "selfish" is too vague or ambiguous. The first premise isn't true. What is true, perhaps, is "If you don't give to charity when you have more money than you need for your essentials, then you're selfish."*

For Exercises 9–23, fill in after the italics.

9. Mr. Ensign is a congressman who shows up for every vote. If someone is a good congressman, he shows up for every vote in congress. So Mr. Ensign is a good congressman.

Argument? (yes or no)
Conclusion:

Premises:

Additional premises needed to make it valid or strong (if none, say so):

Classify: valid   very strong ——————— weak
One of the forms we studied in this chapter? (state which one)
Good argument? (Choose one with an explanation.)
> It's good (passes the three tests).
> It's valid or strong, but you don't know if the premises are true, so you can't say
> if it's good or bad.
> It's bad because it's unrepairable (state which of the reasons apply).

10. Tom: Dick said he would go to the basketball game only if he could get a free ticket.
    Harry: I see he's at the game.
    Tom: He must have gotten a free ticket.

Argument? (yes or no)
Conclusion:

Premises:

Additional premises needed to make it valid or strong (if none, say so):

Classify: valid   very strong ——————— weak

One of the forms we studied in this chapter? (state which one)
Good argument? (Choose one with an explanation.)
> It's good (passes the three tests).
> It's valid or strong, but you don't know if the premises are true, so you can't say
> if it's good or bad.
> It's bad because it's unrepairable (state which of the reasons apply).

11. Dick: If Freud was right, then the only things that matter to a man are fame, riches,
    and the love of beautiful women.
    Zoe: But Ralph is poor, single, never married and uninterested in women (or men),
    and certainly not famous. Yet he's happy. So Freud was wrong.

Argument? (yes or no)
Conclusion:
Premises:

Additional premises needed to make it valid or strong (if none, say so):

Classify: valid   very strong ——————— weak
One of the forms we studied in this chapter? (state which one)
Good argument? (Choose one with an explanation.)
>   It's good (passes the three tests).
>   It's valid or strong, but you don't know if the premises are true, so you can't say
>   if it's good or bad.
>   It's bad because it's unrepairable (state which of the reasons apply).

12. Dick: If Tom isn't a football player, then Suzy won't go out with Tom.
    Zoe: But Suzy went to the movies with Tom.
    Dick: So I guess Tom is a football player.

Argument? (yes or no)
Conclusion:

Premises:

Additional premises needed to make it valid or strong (if none, say so):

Classify: valid   very strong ——————— weak
One of the forms we studied in this chapter? (state which one)
Good argument? (Choose one with an explanation.)
>   It's good (passes the three tests).
>   It's valid or strong, but you don't know if the premises are true, so you can't say
>   if it's good or bad.
>   It's bad because it's unrepairable (state which of the reasons apply).

13. Only if Columbus landed in a place with no people in it could you say that he discovered
    it. But the Americas, especially where he landed, were populated. He even met natives.
    So Columbus didn't discover America. He just discovered a route to America.

Argument? (yes or no)
Conclusion:

Premises:

Additional premises needed to make it valid or strong (if none, say so):

Classify: valid   very strong ——————— weak

One of the forms we studied in this chapter? (state which one)
Good argument? (Choose one with an explanation.)
> It's good (passes the three tests).
> It's valid or strong, but you don't know if the premises are true, so you can't say if it's good or bad.
> It's bad because it's unrepairable (state which of the reasons apply).

14. Tom: If Dick loves Zoe, he'll give her an engagement ring.
    Harry: But Dick loves Spot a lot more than Zoe.
    Suzy: So Dick won't give Zoe an engagement ring.

Argument? (yes or no)
Conclusion:

Premises:

Additional premises needed to make it valid or strong (if none, say so):

Classify: valid   very strong ——————— weak
One of the forms we studied in this chapter? (state which one)
Good argument? (Choose one with an explanation.)
> It's good (passes the three tests).
> It's valid or strong, but you don't know if the premises are true, so you can't say if it's good or bad.
> It's bad because it's unrepairable (state which of the reasons apply).

15. Maria: Professor, professor, why wouldn't you answer my question in class?
    Professor Zzzyzzx: I do not allow questions in my class. If I allow one student to ask a question, then I must allow others, too. Und then I vill have lots and lots of questions to answer. Und I won't have time for my lecture.

Argument? (yes or no)
Conclusion:

Premises:

Additional premises needed to make it valid or strong (if none, say so):

Classify: valid   very strong ——————— weak
One of the forms we studied in this chapter? (state which one)
Good argument? (Choose one with an explanation.)

It's good (passes the three tests).

It's valid or strong, but you don't know if the premises are true, so you can't say
   if it's good or bad.

It's bad because it's unrepairable (state which of the reasons apply).

16. Zoe: This critical thinking book by Epstein is great. If you have a sense of humor you
      should buy it.

    Dick: Even if you don't have a sense of humor, you should buy Epstein's book.

    Tom: So I should buy Epstein's book.

Argument? (yes or no)

Conclusion:

Premises:

Additional premises needed to make it valid or strong (if none, say so):

Classify: valid   very strong ——————— weak

One of the forms we studied in this chapter? (state which one)

Good argument? (Choose one with an explanation.)

   It's good (passes the three tests).

   It's valid or strong, but you don't know if the premises are true, so you can't say
      if it's good or bad.

   It's bad because it's unrepairable (state which of the reasons apply).

17. We shouldn't require uniforms in public schools. No one will like them. If you're poor,
    you'll resent having to spend the extra money on them. If you're rich, you'll resent not
    being able to flaunt your wealth.

Argument? (yes or no)

Conclusion:

Premises:

Additional premises needed to make it valid or strong (if none, say so):

Classify: valid   very strong ——————— weak

One of the forms we studied in this chapter? (state which one)

Good argument? (Choose one with an explanation.)

   It's good (passes the three tests).

   It's valid or strong, but you don't know if the premises are true, so you can't say
      if it's good or bad.

   It's bad because it's unrepairable (state which of the reasons apply).

18. If Dick has a class and Zoe is working, there's no point in calling their home to ask them over for dinner. Spot can't answer the phone.

    Argument? (yes or no)

    Conclusion:

    Premises:

    Additional premises needed to make it valid or strong (if none, say so):

    Classify: valid   very strong ——————— weak

    One of the forms we studied in this chapter? (state which one)

    Good argument? (Choose one with an explanation.)

       It's good (passes the three tests).

       It's valid or strong, but you don't know if the premises are true, so you can't say
          if it's good or bad.

       It's bad because it's unrepairable (state which of the reasons apply).

19. Gun control should not be allowed. If laws requiring registration of all guns are passed, then they'll start investigating people who have guns. They'll tap our phones. They'll look at what we check out of the library. They'll tap our Internet records. It'll be a police state.

    Argument? (yes or no)

    Conclusion:

    Premises:

    Additional premises needed to make it valid or strong (if none, say so):

    Classify: valid   very strong ——————— weak

    One of the forms we studied in this chapter? (state which one)

    Good argument? (Choose one with an explanation.)

       It's good (passes the three tests).

       It's valid or strong, but you don't know if the premises are true, so you can't say
          if it's good or bad.

       It's bad because it's unrepairable (state which of the reasons apply).

20. If murder is the killing of someone with the intent to kill that person, and if Jeffrey Dahmer really did kill all those people they say he did, then, since it seems clear that he would have had to intend to kill them, Jeffrey Dahmer was guilty of murder.

    Argument? (yes or no)

Conclusion:

Premises:

Additional premises needed to make it valid or strong (if none, say so):

Classify: valid   very strong ——————— weak
One of the forms we studied in this chapter? (state which one)
Good argument? (Choose one with an explanation.)
    It's good (passes the three tests).
    It's valid or strong, but you don't know if the premises are true, so you can't say
       if it's good or bad.
    It's bad because it's unrepairable (state which of the reasons apply).

21. Dick: I heard that Tom's going to get a pet. I wonder what he'll get?
    Zoe: The only pets you're allowed in this town are dogs or cats or fish.
    Dick: Well, I know he can't stand cats.
    Zoe: So he'll get a dog or fish.
    Dick: Not fish, he isn't the kind to get a pet you just contemplate.
    Zoe: So let's surprise him and get him a leash.
    Argument? (yes or no)
    Conclusion:
    Premises:

Additional premises needed to make it valid or strong (if none, say so):

Classify: valid   very strong ——————— weak
One of the forms we studied in this chapter? (state which one)
Good argument? (Choose one with an explanation.)
    It's good (passes the three tests).
    It's valid or strong, but you don't know if the premises are true, so you can't say
       if it's good or bad.
    It's bad because it's unrepairable (state which of the reasons apply).

22. Every criminal is either already a hardened repeat offender or will become one because of what he'll learn in jail. We don't want any hardened criminals running free on our streets. So if you lock up someone, he should be locked up forever.

Argument? (yes or no)
Conclusion:

Premises:

Additional premises needed to make it valid or strong (if none, say so):

Classify: valid   very strong ———————— weak
One of the forms we studied in this chapter? (state which one)
Good argument? (Choose one with an explanation.)
　　It's good (passes the three tests).
　　It's valid or strong, but you don't know if the premises are true, so you can't say
　　　if it's good or bad.
　　It's bad because it's unrepairable (state which of the reasons apply).

23. Aid to third world countries? Why should we care more about starving children there
    than here?
    Argument? (yes or no)
    Conclusion:

    Premises:

    Additional premises needed to make it valid or strong (if none, say so):

    Classify: valid   very strong ———————— weak
    One of the forms we studied in this chapter? (state which one)
    Good argument? (Choose one with an explanation.)
    　　It's good (passes the three tests).
    　　It's valid or strong, but you don't know if the premises are true, so you can't say
    　　　if it's good or bad.
    　　It's bad because it's unrepairable (state which of the reasons apply).

24. You've worked hard enough. Take some time off. Go to a bar or a party or a church
    social. Listen. And bring back examples of the valid and invalid forms of reasoning
    we studied in this chapter.

Writing Lesson 8

You've learned about filling in unstated premises, indicator words, what counts as a plausible premise, and reasoning with compound claims.

Write an argument either for or against the following:

> "For any course at this university, if a student attends every class, takes all the exams, and hands in all the assignments, then the professor should give the student a passing mark."

Check whether your instructor has chosen a *DIFFERENT TOPIC* for this assignment.

In order to make sure you use your new skills, the directions for this assignment are a little different. You should hand in two pages.

One page: A list of premises and the conclusion.

One page: The argument written as an essay with indicator words.

We should be able to see at a glance from the list of premises whether your argument is good. The essay form should read just as clearly if you use indicator words well. Remember, there should be no claims in the essay form that aren't listed as premises.

Note that the topic is a conditional. You need to understand how to form the contradictory in order to make up your pro and con lists and to write your argument. Be very clear in your mind about what you consider to be necessary as opposed to sufficient conditions to get a passing mark.

To show you some of the problems my students have, I'm including Suzy's argument on a different topic, as well as Tom's. Lee wrote a better one, so I've included his, too.

Suzy Queue
Critical Thinking

Issue: If a professor's colleagues do not consider his exams to be well written, then marks for the course should be given on a curve, not on percentage.

Premises:

1. A grade on a test reflects just how students are doing on that subject. If a test is not clearly understood, then the reflection of the scores will be lower.

2. Every student deserves to be treated fairly if the test is not clearly written the opportunity is not equal.

3. Due to the unclear test, the grading should start with the highest scored test in the class and the other test scores behind that.

4. Unclear tests should not be given in the first place, so to compensate for the strain on your brain for trying to decipher the test, grades should be curved to compensate.

5. The test is a direct reflection of how the teacher is getting through to his students, so in order to have an accurate idea, grading on the curve would show him the relation of all the students scores together.

Conclusion: Teachers who give poorly written exams should grade on the curve.

A grade on a test reflects just how students are doing on that subject. If the test is not clearly understood, then the reflection of the scores will be lower. Every student deserves to be treated fairly if the test is not clearly written the opportunity is not equal. Due to the unclear test, the grading should start with the highest scored test and the other test score behind that. Unclear tests should not be given in the first place, so to compensate for the strain on your brain for trying to decipher the test, grades should be curved to compensate. The test is a direct reflection of how the teacher is getting through to his students, so in order to have an accurate idea, grading on a curve would show him the relation of all the students scores together. Teachers who give poorly written exams should grade on the curve.

Some serious problems here. For (1), what does "reflect" mean? And "clearly understood"? By whom? That's the point. Besides, it's not one premise—it's two claims. For (2) you apparently have two claims, but it's incoherent. Your (4) is an argument (that word "so" is the clue), not a premise. And (5) is two claims, too.

You almost proved the conclusion you've stated. But you missed the point. It's a lot easier to prove what you stated than the issue you were supposed to write on. Who decides what "poorly written" means? Where is anything about his colleagues?

It's pretty clear to me that you wrote the essay first, and then tried to figure out what you said.

Also, you were supposed to use two pages. And where is your section number?

Tom Wyzyczy
Critical Thinking
Section 4
Writing Lesson 8

Issue: Every student should be required to take either critical thinking or freshman composition, but not both.

Definition: I'll understand the issue as "University students should be required to take either a freshman course on critical thinking or freshman composition, but not both."

Premises:

Critical thinking courses teach how to write. *1*

Freshman composition teaches how to write. *2*

Critical thinking courses teach how to read an essay. *3*

Freshman composition teaches how to read an essay. *4*

Credit should not be given for taking two courses that teach roughly the same material. *5*

If credit shouldn't be given for taking a course, students shouldn't be required to take it. *6*

Conclusion: Every student should be required to take either critical thinking or freshman composition, but not both.

continued on next page

This is sloppy work compared to what you've done in the past. First, the conclusion of your argument is that a student should not have to take both courses. But you haven't shown that he should take one or the other, which is also part of the issue [(A or B) and not C]. So you've established neither the original claim nor its contradictory.

You need a claim that links 1–4 with 5 and 6, like "Freshman composition and critical thinking courses teach the same material." (I see on the next page you do have that claim.)

But worse is that 6 is at best dubious: How about those students who have to take remedial math for which no credit is given? And 1–4 are too vague. Both courses teach "how to write," but quite different aspects of that. Ditto for 3 and 4.

Tom Wyzyczy, writing lesson 8, page 2

Both critical thinking courses and freshman composition courses teach how to write. Both critical thinking courses and freshman composition courses teach how to read an essay. Since they both teach roughly the same material, they shouldn't both be required, because credit should not be given for taking two courses that teach roughly the same material. And if credit shouldn't be given for taking a course, students shouldn't be required to take it.

Good use of indicator words. It was o.k. to put two claims together in the first sentence as you did, since you recognized in your list of premises that they were two claims.

But you did what I specifically asked you not to do. You added a claim here you didn't have on the previous page: "Both courses teach roughly the same material."

The argument looks so plausible when it's written this way, but the previous page shows its weaknesses.

You should re-do this whole assignment.

Lee Hong-Nakamura O'Flanagan

Issue: If critical thinking were not a required course, a lot fewer people would take it.

Definition: I assume that "a lot fewer" is purposely vague.

Premises: ‡ Critical thinking is required of all students now.
‡ Critical thinking is one of the harder core requirement courses.
‡ A lot of students prefer to take easy courses, rather than learn something.
‡ Students in engineering and architecture have more courses to take than they can finish in four years.
‡ Students don't want to spend more time at their studies than they have to.[1]
‡ Money is a problem for many students.[2]
‡ For most students, if they have more courses to take than they can finish in four years, they will not take courses that aren't required.[3]
‡ Students think they already know how to think critically.[4]
‡ If critical thinking weren't required, then students who prefer easy courses and students who want to finish as quickly as they can, which are a lot of students, will not take it.

Conclusion: If critical thinking were not a required course, a lot fewer people would take it.

Critical thinking is required of all students now. And critical thinking is one of the harder core requirement courses. A lot of students prefer to take easy courses, rather than learn something. So many of them won't take critical thinking.[5] Besides, students in engineering and architecture have more courses than they can finish in four years. Why would they take critical thinking if they didn't have to? After all, we all know that students don't want to spend more time at their studies than they have to. After all, money is a problem for most students. So for most students, if they have more courses to take than they can finish in four years, they will not take courses that aren't required. Anyway, students think they already know how to think critically. Thus we can see that if critical thinking weren't required, then students who prefer easy courses and students who want to finish as quickly as they can, which are a lot of students, will not take it. That is, if critical thinking were not a required course, a lot fewer people would take it.

This is good, but there are a few problems. 1 isn't tied into 3, though the unstated premise is pretty clear. But 2 definitely needs to be tied into 3 better. And 4 is left dangling—what's the connection you intend? Finally, you use 5 and it should be on the list of premises.

And DOUBLE SPACE and put your SECTION NUMBER on the sheet!

Writing Lesson 9

For each of the following write the best argument you can that has as conclusion the **claim** below the cartoon. List only the premises and conclusion. If you believe the best **argument** is only weak, explain why.

Do not make up a story about the cartoon. Use what you see in the cartoon **and your** common knowledge.

1.

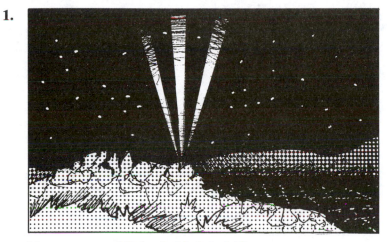

There are searchlights behind the hill.

2.

Someone has walked here since the snow began falling.

3.

This is a school for the handicapped.

4.

Spot escaped by digging a hole under the fence.

Name _____ Section _____

7 Complex Arguments

Key Words   direct ways of refuting   strawman
                     reducing to the absurd   dependent premises
                     ridicule   independent premises

Exercises for Sections A and B

1. In my comment after the argument about bicycling on p. 153 of the text I challenge the student. Have I shown that the argument is bad?

2. What is a counterargument?

3. If you show an argument is bad, what have you shown about its conclusion?

4. How should you respond to a counterargument?

5. a. Why are counterarguments useful in your own writing?

    b. Give three phrases you can use to introduce objections to your own argument in your writing.

6. Find an article in which the author answers a counterargument.

7. Explain the role of each claim in the following discussion.

    Zoe: I think sex is the answer to almost everyone's problems.

    Dick: How can you say that?

    Zoe: It takes away your tensions, right?

    Dick: Not if you're involved with someone you don't like.

    Zoe: Well, anyway, it makes you feel better.

    Dick: Not if it's against your morals. Anyway, heroin makes you feel good, too.

    Zoe: But it's healthy, natural, just like eating and drinking.

    Dick: Sure, and you can catch terrible diseases. Sex should be confined to marriage.

    Zoe: Is that a proposal?

8. Write a short argument against drinking alcohol that acknowledges why some people want to drink alcohol.

9. If you can show that a collection of claims leads to a false conclusion, do you know that the claims are inconsistent or one of them is false? Explain.

10. Refuting an argument directly is just showing that the argument is _____ .

11. What is reducing an argument to the absurd?

12. Which of the ways of refuting an argument is best? Why?

13. What's the difference between ridicule and reducing to the absurd?

14. Why isn't a phony refutation really a refutation of an argument?

15. Why won't a slippery slope argument do as a way to reduce to the absurd?

16. a.. What is a strawman?

    b. Bring in an example from a newspaper or television or magazine.

Evaluate the following attempts to refute arguments by filling in after the italics.

17. There is no value at all in Heidegger's philosophy, especially his ethics, since he collaborated with the Nazis in running German universities in the 1930s, and fired all the Jews.

What is the method of refutation?

Is the refutation a good argument? (Explain)

18. You say you want to raise tuition again? Why not raise the parking fees, too? And the dorm contracts. And raise prices at the cafeteria, while you're at it. Or maybe even charge students for using the library. You could balance the college's budget for sure that way.

What is the method of refutation?

Is the refutation a good argument? (Explain)

19. Look, I agree with you. We have too much violence in the streets, too many drug pushers, too little respect for the law. But our prisons are overflowing, and that's costing us a fortune. So we've got to reduce our prison population. Yet you say we should be even tougher on crime. The answer is simple: Institute a lottery among all convicted felons in jail and execute one of them every month, no appeals. That'll instill a real fear of being arrested. And it'd be fair, too.

What is the method of refutation?

Is the refutation a good argument? (Explain)

20. Lee: I'm going to vote for that initiative to eliminate discrimination against homosexuals in hiring and getting places to live. They should be treated like everyone else. They deserve a chance to get jobs and homes.

   Tom: Are you kidding? I'm voting against it. You should, too. They don't deserve any preference over the rest of us.

What is the method of refutation?

Is the refutation a good argument? (Explain)

Refute the following arguments. Say whether you are showing a premise is dubious, attacking an unstated premise, showing the argument is weak, or reducing to the absurd.

21. Single parents should get special assistance from the government. After all, a two-parent family has two paychecks and twice the attention to give to their children. Some single parent families end up having to use the welfare system because they can't afford child care. Therefore, the government should give free child care to single-parent families.

22. Multiple-choice examinations are the best way to examine students. The grading is completely objective. Students know how to prepare for them. And professors don't have to spend a lot of time grading them.

23. You should keep a gun in your home. This is a dangerous neighborhood, and a gun is the best protection you can get. Think of what could happen if someone broke in.

Exercises for Sections C and D

1. a. What does it mean to say that premises are dependent? Independent?

   b. Can we say that a conclusion is dependent? Explain.

   c. Give an argument all of whose premises are independent.

   d. Repair your argument in (c) by adding premises.

2. Give an example (not from the text) of a strong argument with just one premise supporting a conclusion. That is, no unstated premise is missing. (Hint: Look in Chapter 3.)

I've asked Tom to analyze the structure of a few arguments. Here's some of his work.

The dogcatcher in this town is mean. *1* **He likes to kill dogs.** *2* **He is overzealous, picking up dogs that aren't really strays.** *3* **Some people say he beats the dogs.** *4* **So the position of dogcatcher should be eliminated.** *5*

Argument? (yes or no) Yes.

Conclusion: The position of dogcatcher should be eliminated.

Number the claims

Additional premises needed? If someone likes to kill dogs, picks up dogs that aren't really strays, and beats dogs, then he is mean. *a* If someone is mean, he shouldn't be dogcatcher. *b*

Identify any subargument, saying which claims are independent: 2, 3, and 4 are independent and support *1*. Then *1* supports the conclusion, 5.

Good argument? Looks good to me.

You haven't been critical enough. The argument is really pretty bad. First, I agree that 2, 3, and 4 are independent. You can say they support 1, but 1 is vague and no improvement on 2,

3, and 4. I think it's too vague to be a claim. We do need something like your a . But for that we need a further premise, one you're always overlooking, "If people say that the dogcatcher beats dogs, then he does beat dogs." And that's pretty dubious. So instead of a let's take: "If someone likes to kill dogs and picks up dogs that aren't strays, then he should not be a dogcatcher". That's true. But that doesn't get you the conclusion. What you then need is, "If the person who is now dogcatcher shouldn't be dogcatcher, then the position of dogcatcher should be eliminated." And that is implausible. Still, it's just your first try.

Harry wants to get a dog. *1* **Harry's friends Celia and Emily have puppies they want to give away.** *2* **Celia's is a border collie** *3* **and Emily's is a dalmatian.** *4* **Harry likes border collies better than dalmatians.** *5* **So he'll probably take Celia's puppy.** *6*

Argument? (yes or no) Yes.

Conclusion: Harry will probably take Celia's puppy.

Additional premises needed? If Harry wants to get a dog, then he'll get one of his friends' puppies.

Identify any subargument, saying which claims are independent: *1, 2, 3, 4,* and *5* are independent and support the conclusion, *6.*

Good argument? Very strong, and I know the premises are true. So it's good.

Much better. The conclusion, however, doesn't have the word "probably" in it—that's an indicator word.

You're still having trouble identifying what's dependent. Look, 3, 4, and 5 work together to support an unstated claim: "If Harry picks one of Celia or Emily's puppies, it'll be Celia's." Then that plus the unstated premise you added make the argument moderately strong. Perhaps some other friend has puppies to give away, too.

3. Dr. E is a teacher. All teachers are men. So Dr. E is a man.

    Argument? (yes or no)

    If an argument, number each part that might be a claim.

    Conclusion:

    Additional premises needed?

    Identify any subargument, stating which claims are dependent:

    Good argument?

4. Sheep are the dumbest animals. If the one in front walks off a cliff, all the rest will follow him. And if they get rolled over on their backs, they can't right themselves.

    Argument? (yes or no)

    If an argument, number each part that might be a claim.

    Conclusion:

    Additional premises needed?

Identify any subargument, stating which claims are dependent:

Good argument?

5. I'm on my way to school. I left five minutes late. Traffic is heavy. Therefore, I'll be late for class. So I might as well stop and get breakfast.
    Argument? (yes or no)
    If an argument, number each part that might be a claim.
    Conclusion:

    Additional premises needed?

    Identify any subargument, stating which claims are dependent:

    Good argument?

6. Pigs are very intelligent animals. They make great pets. They learn to do tricks as well as any dog can. They can be housetrained, too. And they are affectionate, since they like to cuddle. Pigs are known as one of the smartest animals there are. And if you get bored with them or they becomes unruly, you can eat them.
    Argument? (yes or no)
    If an argument, number each part that might be a claim.
    Conclusion:

    Additional premises needed?

    Identify any subargument, stating which claims are dependent:

    Good argument?

7. Smoking is disgusting. It makes your breath smell horrid. If you've ever kissed someone after they smoked a cigarette you feel as though you're going to vomit. Besides, it will kill you.
    Argument? (yes or no)
    If an argument, number each part that might be a claim.
    Conclusion:

Additional premises needed?

Identify any subargument, stating which claims are dependent:

Good argument?

8.   Dr. E: I took my dogs for a walk last night in the fields behind my house. It was very dark. They started to chase something: I could hear it running in front of them. It seemed like it was big because of the way the bushes were rustling, and they came back towards where I was in a U turn, which suggests it wasn't a rabbit. Rabbits almost always run in more or less one direction. I think they killed it, because I heard a funny squeaky "awk" sound. It didn't sound like a cat, but it didn't sound like a big animal either. And I don't think rabbits make that kind of sound.   I'm puzzled what it was, but one thing I am sure of after the dogs returned: It wasn't a skunk.

Argument? (yes or no)
If an argument, number each part that might be a claim.
Conclusion:

Additional premises needed?

Identify any subargument, stating which claims are dependent:

Good argument?

9.   Las Vegas has too many people. There's not enough water in the desert to support more than a million people. And the infrastructure of the city can't handle more than a million: The streets are overcrowded and traffic is always congested; the schools are overcrowded and new ones can't be built fast enough. We should stop migration to the city by tough zoning laws in the city and county.

Argument? (yes or no)
If an argument, number each part that might be a claim.
Conclusion:

Additional premises needed?

Identify any subargument, stating which claims are dependent:

Good argument?

10. (Charlie Graven speaking on Geraldo about Nicole Simpson calling 911 and not
    following up on it)
    She didn't file charges, she didn't get a restraining order, therefore . . . If I were
    getting harassed, I would file charges, I would get a restraining order.

Argument? (yes or no)

If an argument, number each part that might be a claim.

Conclusion:

Additional premises needed?

Identify any subargument, stating which claims are dependent:

Good argument?

Name _____ Section _____

Exercises for Section E

1. On pp. 239–241 of the text Tom has tried his hand at analyzing a long argument. Though it uses a few ideas from Chapter 9, it ought to be clear enough. Read through it and say if he's followed the steps for analysis given in Section E.

2. Finish the analysis of the first argument of this section.

3. Find an editorial or a letter to the editor from your local newspaper and analyze it.

4. Here is the reply to Betsy Hart by Bonnie Erbe that appeared in the same feature. Analyze it.

Bonnie Erbe: Before my colleague takes off on such wild tangents, she needs to define affirmative action. The term has come to mean different things to different people, ranging from strict, unbending quotas to mild incentive programs.

My definition of affirmative action is as follows: institutions and corporations that have extremely small percentages of women and/or minority group members among their ranks should take gender and race into account, along with a panoply of other factors (i.e., intelligence, job or grade performance, geographic distribution, economic disadvantage) when recruiting new talent.

Using that definition, affirmative action will undoubtedly be outmoded in some institutions, but decidedly necessary in others.

For example, there's clearly no need to pay special attention to admit more Chinese- or Japanese-Americans to the University of California at Berkeley.

But blacks and Hispanics are still underrepresented on some campuses in the University of California system.

Similarly, some federal agencies–most notably the FBI, the CIA and the State Department–are woefully short on women agents and diplomats. Yet the Justice Department's No. 1 and No. 2 lawyers (Janet Reno and Jamie Gorelick) are women. Hence, affirmative action for women is unneeded in some federal agencies, while not in others.

Besides, if we are going to eliminate affirmative action entirely, we ought to eliminate all preferences throughout society.

No more special admissions to Harvard for the young man with a B minus average just because his grandfather's name is on a Harvard dorm.

Fathers should no longer be able to hire sons (or sons-in-law) to help run the family company simply because they're related.

I'm being hyperbolic, but my point is this: Preferences (based on who you know and how much money you have) are still rampant in society. If we eliminate one, in fairness we should eliminate them all.

If we actually, really eliminated preferences–all forms of affirmative action–upper-class white children would be much more thoroughly vitiated than lower-class minority children.

Scripps Howard News Service

Writing Lesson 10

Now you know that you should include the other side when arguing for a controversial claim. Argument, counterargument, counter-counterargument. Remember, to knock off an objection, you need a mini-argument that will be judged by the same standards as any argument.

Write an argument either for or against the following:

"Students in public high schools should be required to wear uniforms."

Check whether your instructor has chosen a *DIFFERENT TOPIC* for this assignment.

In order to make sure you use your new skills, the directions for this assignment are the same as for Writing Lesson 6. You should hand in two pages:

One page: A list of premises and the conclusion.

One page: The argument written as an essay with indicator words.

We should be able to see at a glance from the list of premises whether your argument is good. The essay form should read just as clearly, if you use indicator words well. Remember, there should be no claims in the essay form that aren't listed as premises. And you should include the other side.

For this issue and generally, there is a trade-off: You can make your argument very strong, but perhaps only at the expense of a rather dubious premise. Or you can make all your premises clearly true, but leave out the dubious premises that are needed to make the argument strong. Given the choice, *opt for making the argument strong*. If it's weak, no one should accept the conclusion. And if it's weak because of unstated premises, it is better to have those premises stated so they can be the object of debate.

Tom's so embarrassed about his last writing assignment that he's asked me not to include any more. But he's doing much better now, and I'm sure he'll do well in the course. Maria's done such a good job, though, that I'm including her essay on a different issue.

Maria Schwartz Rodriguez
Critical Thinking, Section 6
Writing Lesson 10

Issue: If a woman has a baby, then she should not work outside the home until the child reaches the age of four.

Definition: I take "work outside the home" to mean the woman takes a job that requires her to be away from her home and child at least 15 hours/week.

Premises:

1. Some women who have a child under the age of four are single mothers.

2. Some women who have a child under the age of four have husbands who do not earn enough money to support them and the child.

3. Some women who have children have careers from which they cannot take time without stopping them permanently or for a very long time from advancing.

4. Some women who have children do not have extended families or lots of friends.

5. A woman who has only her family can go stir-crazy if she is just with her child all the time.

6. A woman who is going stir-crazy, or who is too poor to provide for her child, or is unsatisfied because her child is stopping her from getting along in her career will make a bad mother and companion for her child who is under four.

7. Mothers who are not with their children do not deserve to have children.

8. Whether they deserve to have them or not, they do have them.

9. Children who are not with their mothers will not develop proper intellectual and emotional skills.

10. What studies I have seen contradict that claim. Until reliable studies are produced for it, we should not accept it.

11. Day-care can be dangerous.

12. The mother can screen day-care providers, and besides, a bitter, unsatisfied mother can be dangerous, too.

Conclusion: Under some circumstances it is acceptable for a woman to work outside the home when she has a child under the age of four.

Maria Schwartz Rodriguez
Critical Thinking, Section 6
Writing Lesson 10, page 2

Under some circumstances it is acceptable for a woman to work outside the home when she has a child under the age of four. After all, some women who have a child under the age of four are single mothers. And other women who have a child under the age of four have husbands who do not earn enough money to support them and the child. We can't forget women who have children and have careers from which they cannot take time without stopping them permanently or for a very long time from advancing. And think of the women who have children who do not have extended families or lots of friends. She could go stir-crazy if she is just with her child all the time.   These women should be allowed to take work outside the home, for a woman who is going stir-crazy, or who is too poor to provide for her child, or is unsatisfied because her child is stopping her from getting along in her career will make a bad mother and companion for her child who is under four.

But lots of people say that mothers who are not with their children do not deserve to have children. Well, whether they deserve to have them or not, they do have them.

But children who aren't with their mothers will not develop proper intellectual and emotional skills, it is said. Well, what studies I have seen contradict that claim. Until reliable studies are produced for it, we should not accept it.

One objection is that mothers who work outside the home often need day-care.*A* And day-care can be dangerous. But the mother can screen day-care providers, and besides, a bitter, unsatisfied mother can be dangerous, too.

So despite the obvious objections, we can see that under some circumstances it is acceptable for a woman to work outside the home when she has a child under the age of four.

This is really excellent. Bravo! A few points where you could improve:

You must include the definition in the essay, right after the first sentence giving the conclusion.

The grammar on premise 3 is not right.

You missed a possible response to 8 that the state or a church should take the child, and you'd need to come up with a response to that.

Some variety in putting in the objections might be good, for example, stating (9) as a question.

You left A out of your list of premises. And (12) is two premises, not one.

I see you avoided entirely the issue of welfare. Have you asked other students to look at your paper to see if they can think of objections or support because of that?

If you can write like this in your other courses you'll do great all through college!

8 General Claims

Key Words all

        some

        universal claim

        existential claim

        contradictory

        negative universal claim

        only

        direct way of reasoning
          with "all"

        arguing backwards with "all"

reasoning in a chain with "all"

direct way of reasoning with "no"

arguing backwards with "no"

reasoning in a chain with "some"

precise generalities

vague generalities

direct way of reasoning with
    "almost all"

arguing backwards with "almost all"

Exercises for Sections A–C

1. Give three other ways to say "All cars use gasoline."

2. Give three other ways to say "Some dogs bark."

3. Give two other ways to say "All students are smart."

4. Give three other ways to say "Some women are married."

5.   Give at least one other way to say "Only birds fly."

6.   Give three other ways to say "No teacher is illiterate."

7.   Give another way to say "Everything that's a dog is a domestic canine and everything that's a domestic canine is a dog."

8.   Give two other ways to say "No pig can fly."

9.   What is a universal claim?

10. What is an existential claim?

11. What is a negative universal claim?

Judging from your experience, which of the following are true? Be prepared to defend your answer.

12. Only dogs bark.

13. All blondes are dumb.

14. Some cars are designed to fall apart after six years.

15. Crest toothpaste is not available in all supermarkets.

16. Some critical thinking professors are women.

17. Every outhouse is made of wood.

18. Dictionaries are the only way to learn the meaning of new words.

19. No student can register for this course after the first week of classes.

For Exercises 20–40 give a contradictory claim.

20. All dogs bark.

21. No teacher is friendly.

22. Some dogs bite mailmen.

23. Every cat has clawed its owner.

24. Some rats aren't unpleasant.

25. Cat owners need regular physical examinations.

26. No dog owner is truly unhappy.

27. If some dog owner likes cats, then he or she is mentally unbalanced.

28. This exam will be given in all of the sections of critical thinking.

29. No exam is suitable for all students.

30. Some exams don't really test a student's knowledge.

31. Not all foxes are red.

32. Students who play up to their teachers get good grades.

33. Only philosophy professors know how to teach critical thinking.

34. All policemen and only policemen carry guns.

35. Nothing both barks and meows.

36. These exercises are boring.

37. Every subscriber to this magazine is gullible.

38. Decisions about abortion should be left to the woman and her doctor.

39. The Lone Ranger was the only cowboy to have a friend called "Tonto."

40. Only Dr. E, of all teachers, knows how to bark.

Here are two examples of how Maria and Lee have been using the diagrams to check for validity. They'll help you with the exercises for Section D.

Exercises for Section D

Which of the argument forms in Exercises 1–6 are valid? Justify your answer. Then give an argument of that form.

1. All S are P.
   No Q is S.
   So some Q aren't P.

2. All S are P.
   a is S.
   So *a* is P.

3. Some S are P.
   All P are Q.
   So some S are Q.

4. Only S are P.
   a is S.
   So *a* is P.

5. Some S aren't P.
   So no P are S.

6. All S are P.
   No Q is P.
   So no Q is S.

For exercises 7–13, select the claim that makes the argument valid. (Don't judge whether the claim is plausible, just whether it makes the argument valid.)

7. All turtles can swim. So turtles eat fish.

    a. Anything that eats fish swims.
    b. Fish swim and are eaten by things that swim.
    c. Anything that swims eats fish.
    d. None of the above.

8. Every teacher at this school gets a free parking space. So Ms. Fletcher is a teacher at this school.

    a. Ms. Fletcher has a free parking space at this school.
    b. Ms. Fletcher is at this school every day.
    c. Both (a) and (b).
    d. None of the above.

9. Dogs bark. So dogs eat meat.

    a. Anything that eats meat barks.
    b. Dogs don't meow.
    c. Anything that barks eats meat.
    d. None of the above.

10. All heroin addicts cannot function in a 9–5 job. So no one who teaches is a heroin addict.

    a. Teachers usually don't take drugs.
    b. Teachers can work hard.
    c. All teachers can function in a 9–5 job.
    d. None of the above.

11. Every policeman must pass a physical fitness examination. So no person with heart-disease can pass a physical fitness examination.

    a. No person with heart-disease is a policeman.
    b. No person with heart-disease is physically fit.
    c. If you're a policeman, you can pass a physical fitness exam.
    d. None of the above.

12. Some dogs chase cats. So some cats are bitten.

    a. Some dogs catch cats.
    b. Some things that chase cats bite them.
    c. Some dogs bite cats.
    d. None of the above.

13. Every dog chases cats. So Spot chases Puff.

    a. Spot is a dog.
    b. Puff is a cat.
    c. Puff irritates Spot.
    d. Both (a) and (b).
    e. None of the above.

Which of Exercises 14–31 are valid arguments? (You are not expected to determine whether it is good, only whether it is valid.) Check by doing *one* of the following:

- Give an example in which the premises are true and conclusion false.
- Draw a diagram.
- Point out that the argument is in one of the forms we have studied.
- Explain in your own words why it's valid.

14. Not every student attends lectures. Zoe is a student. So Zoe doesn't attend lectures.

15. No students are enthusiastic about mathematics. Dr. E is not a student. So Dr. E is enthusiastic about mathematics.

16. No students are enthusiastic about mathematics. Harry is enthusiastic about mathematics. So Harry is not a student.

17. Some dogs bite mailmen. Some mailmen bite dogs. So some dogs and mailmen bite each other.

18. Everyone who is anxious to learn works hard. Dr. E's students work hard. So Dr. E's students are anxious to learn.

19. All lions are fierce, but some lions are afraid of dogs. So some dogs aren't afraid of lions.

20. All students who are serious take critical thinking in their freshman year. No heroin addict is a serious student. So no heroin addict takes critical thinking his freshman year.

21. No student who cheats is honest. Some dishonest people are found out. So some students who cheat are found out.

22. Some people who like pizza are vegetarians. Some vegetarians will not eat eggs. So some people who like pizza will not eat eggs.

23. Only ducks quack. George is a duck. So George quacks.

24. Everyone who likes ducks likes quackers. Dick likes ducks. Dick likes cheese. So Dick likes cheese and quackers.

25. No dogcatcher is kind. Anyone who's kind loves dogs. So no dogcatcher loves dogs.

26. Some things that grunt are hogs. Some hogs are good to eat. So some things that grunt are good to eat.

27. Every newspaper Dr. E reads is published by an American publisher. All newspapers published by an American publisher are biased against Muslims. So Dr. E reads only newspapers that are biased against Muslims.

28. Not every canary can sing. So some canaries can sing.

29. Some art students aren't good at math. John is an art student. So John isn't good at math.

30. Every dog loves its master. Dr. E has a dog. So Dr. E is loved.

31. Every cat sheds hair on its master's clothes. Dr. E does not have a cat. So Dr. E has no cat hair shed on his clothes.

32. Arguing backwards with "all" and arguing backwards with conditionals are related. We can rewrite:

All dogs bark.		If anything is a dog, then it barks.
Ralph barks.	as	Ralph barks.
So Ralph is a dog.		So Ralph is a dog.

Rewrite the following universal claims as conditionals:

All good teachers give fair exams.

Every horse loves attention.

Ducks like water.

Exercises for Section E

1. Give two other ways to say, "Almost all dogs bark."

2. Give two other ways to say, "Only a few cats bark."

Which of the argument forms in Exercises 3–6 are strong? Justify your answer.

3. Very few S are P.
    a is S.
    So *a* is not P.

4. Very few S are P.
    a is P.
    So *a* is not S.

5. Most S are P.
    Most P are Q.
    So most S are Q.

6. Almost all S are P.
   Every P is Q.
   So almost all S are Q.

Which of the following arguments are strong? Check by doing one of the following:
  - Give enough examples in which the premises are true and conclusion false.
  - Point out that the argument is in one of the forms we have studied.
  - Explain in your own words why it's strong or weak.

7. Very few college students use heroin. Zoe is a college student. So Zoe doesn't use heroin.

8. Almost no students are enthusiastic about mathematics. Harry is enthusiastic about mathematics. So Harry is not a student.

9. Only a very few dogs like cats. Almost no cats like dogs. So virtually no dogs and cats like each other.

10. A majority of people who are anxious to learn work hard. Dr. E's students work hard. So a majority of Dr. E's students are anxious to learn.

11. No student who cheats is honest. Almost all dishonest people are found out. So almost all students who cheat are found out.

12. Almost all people who are vegetarians like pizza. Almost all vegetarians will not eat eggs. So all but a few people who like pizza will not eat eggs.

13. Mostly ducks quack. George is a duck. So George quacks.

14. Most things that grunt are hogs. Almost all hogs are good to eat. So most things that grunt are good to eat.

15. All but a very few canaries can sing. So not many canaries can't sing.

16. Very few art students are good at math. John is an art student. So John isn't good at math.

17. Almost every dog loves its master. Dr. E has a dog. So Dr. E is loved.

Writing Lesson 11

Write an argument either for or against the following:

> "All students at this school who are physically able should be required to take a course in physical education."

Check whether your instructor has chosen a *DIFFERENT TOPIC* for this assignment.

The issue is simple. There's nothing subtle that you're supposed to do here that you haven't done on the previous assignments. You just need to know how to argue for or against a universal claim. And for that you must be sure you can form the contradictory of it.

By now you should have learned a lot about writing arguments. You don't need more examples, just practice using the new ideas presented in the chapters. You can use as a guide Composing Good Arguments at the end of the text (p. 339), which summarizes many of the lessons you've learned.

Review Exercises for Chapters 6–8

1. What is an argument?

2. What is the definition of a "good argument"?

3. What is a valid argument?

4. What does it mean to say an argument is strong?

5. Is every valid argument good? Explain.

6. How do you show an argument is not valid?

7. Is every valid or strong argument with true premises good? Explain.

8. What is a compound claim?

9. a.   What is a conditional?

    b.   Give an example, then rewrite it four ways, one of which uses "only if."

10. a.   What is a contradictory of a claim?

    b.   Give an example of an "or" claim and its contradictory.

    c.   Give an example of a conditional and its contradictory.

    d.   Give an example of an "only if" claim and its contradictory.

11. Give an example of arguing by excluding possibilities. Is it valid?

12. What is a false dilemma? Give an example.

13. Give an example of the direct way of reasoning with conditionals. Is it valid?

14. Give an example of the indirect way of reasoning with conditionals. Is it valid?

15. Give an example of affirming the consequent. Is it valid?

16. Give an example of denying the antecedent. Is it valid?

17. Is every argument that uses reasoning in a chain with conditionals good? Explain.

18. a.   What does it mean to say that A is a necessary condition for B?

    b.   Give examples of claims A and B such that:
         i.   A is necessary for B, but A is not sufficient for B

         ii.   A is sufficient for B, but A is not necessary for B

         iii. A is both necessary and sufficient for B

         iv.   A is neither necessary nor sufficient for B

19. Why is it a good idea to include a counterargument to an argument that you are writing?

20. What are the three ways of directly refuting an argument?

21. When you use the method of reducing to the absurd to refute an argument, does it show that one of the premises is false?

22. Give an example of a phony refutation.

23. How does a slippery slope argument differ from reducing to the absurd?

24. How does ridicule differ from reducing to the absurd?

25. a.   What is a universal claim?

    b.   Give an example and a contradictory of it.

26. a.   What is an existential claim?

    b.   Give an example and a contradictory of it.

27. Give an example of arguing backwards with "all." Is it valid?

28. Give an "only" claim and rewrite it as a universal claim.

29. Give an example of a strong method of reasoning with vague generalities.

30. Give an example of a weak method of reasoning with vague generalities.

31. List the valid forms of arguments we studied.

32. List the invalid forms we said indicated that an argument is not repairable.

33. List the strong forms of argument we studied.

34. List the weak forms of argument we said indicated an argument is not repairable.

9   Concealed Claims

Key Words

slanter	downplayer	weaseler
loaded question	up-player	proof substitute
euphemism	hyperbole	burden of proof
dysphemism	qualifier	innuendo

Exercises for Chapter 9

1. a. Why is it wrong to use a persuasive definition?

    b. Give an example (not from the text) of a persuasive definition. What claim(s)
        is it concealing?

2. Come up with a loaded question you might pose to an instructor to try to make him or
    her give you a better grade.

3. Give a loaded question you might ask a policeman when he stops you.

4.   Give an example of politically correct language and rephrase it in neutral language.

5.   Give a euphemism and a dysphemism for each of the following. Be sure your word or phrase can be used in a sentence in place of the original.
   a.   Used car

   b.   Sexually explicit books

   c.   Cat

   d.   Handicapped person

   e.   Unemployed

6.   Bring in an example of a euphemism from a network news broadcast.

7.   Bring in an example of a dysphemism from a network news broadcast.

8.   Bring in an example of a downplayer. Say what the hidden claim is.

9.   Bring in an example of hyperbole from a network news broadcast.

10. Typical proof substitutes are "Obviously," "Everyone knows that . . ." List six more.

11. Bring in an example from *another* textbook in which it sounds like the author is giving an argument but there's really no proof.

12. Bring in an example from a political speech in which it sounds like the speaker is giving an argument but there's really no proof.

13. Write a neutral description of someone you know well, one that a third party could use to recognize him or her. Now write a slanted version by replacing the neutral terms with euphemisms and/or dysphemisms, adding downplayers or up-players.

Neutral

Slanted

14. Rewrite the following in neutral language. All are actual quotes.
    a. "The president misspoke himself."
        (Attributed to Ron Ziegler, press secretary for Richard Nixon)

    b. "Our operatives succeeded with the termination with extreme prejudice."
        (Reported by the CIA)

    c. "There was a premature impact of the aircraft with the terrain below."
        (Announced by the FAA)

Say what, if anything, is wrong with the following. Make any concealed claim explicit:

15. Dick: That was really rotten, making me wait for an hour.
    Zoe: I'm sorry you feel that way.

16. I was only three miles over the speed limit, officer.

17. (Ron Ziegler was the press secretary for Richard Nixon's administration.)
    Ziegler: So it was a really terrific year except for the downside.
    Interviewer: What downside?
    Ziegler: Watergate.

18. Can't you ever get to class on time?

19. Lee: I used to find Peruvian women attractive, until I learned Spanish.

20. Those hippies are protesting the war again.

21. Students should be required to wear uniforms in high schools. It has been well documented that wearing uniforms reduces gang violence.

22. A book on Hopi prophecies by a former Lutheran minister [Rev. Thomas Mails] has reignited a battle between tribal members and the author about the sanctity of his actions.
    Mails claims he and Evehema recently deciphered a symbol on an ancient Hopi stone tablet that revealed the next world war will be started by China at an undisclosed time.
    "If what they told me is true, it's the most important message in the world today," Mails said.

    Associated Press, in *The Spectrum,* September 30, 1996

23. Why won't those tree huggers let us get on with logging?

24. Did you hear that the lumber company is planning to cut down the forest?

25. I'm surprised your readers took offense at the truth.

26. The gaming industry in Nevada recorded another record year of profits.

27. Your instructor teaches pretty well for someone his (her) age.

28. Probably your instructor just forgot to write down your grade. Certainly she wouldn't have lied to you about it.

29. An alcoholic is someone with a lack of willpower to stop drinking alcohol.

30. Tom: Hey Dr. E, did you read in the newspaper what Madonna said after she had her first child this week? "This is the greatest miracle that's ever happened to me."

   Dr. E: The biggest miracle that ever happened to Madonna is that she had a career in music.

31. The so-called reform in taxes is nothing more than a redistribution of wealth from the poor to the rich.

32. That corporation wants to erect a hotel in an unspoiled wilderness area.

33. I'm sorry to hear your dog passed away.

34. (Catcatcher) Hey, lady, I'm paid to terminate cats.

35. Doctors are just legal drug-pushers.

36. **Experts say too many get too little sleep**

   Many Americans will happily snooze through the extra hour provided by Sunday's shift into daylight-saving time.

   But researchers say the annual luxury scarcely dents the national sleep deficit. Too many Americans are on the verge of nodding off.

   "I think most experts would agree that self-imposed sleep deprivation is a major problem for many people," said Mark Chambers, a psychologist and clinical director of The Sleep Clinic of Nevada in Las Vegas. "Sleep seems to be the lowest priority on people's list."

   Charlotte Huff, *Las Vegas Review-Journal,* October, 1996

37. The National Rifle Association intends to arm every man, woman, and child in this country. Only by forcefully countering their arguments can we stop these gun-pushers from destroying our society.

38. Those ACLU freaks will defend anyone: They even defended the free-speech rights of Nazis in Chicago.

39. That male chauvinist pig won't stop "complimenting" me.

40. What's a nurse? A nurse is someone who does the doctor's job, cleans up after his messes, and gets paid a tenth of what he gets paid.

41. The United States has no plans at present for invading Cuba.

42. Alan Boss, an astronomer at the Carnegie Institution in Washington D.C., remarked on the discovery of a large planet orbiting a nearby star: "It's a very nice discovery. Even a single discovery like this can make people stop and rethink everything that's happened so far."

43. (Headline for AP story by Marc Rice, *The Spectrum*, October 29, 1996, concerning the guard, Richard Jewell, who discovered the bomb at the Olympics)
    No Hard Evidence Linking Jewell to Olympic bombing

44. The county sanitation workers are threatening to go out on strike.

45. At last our government has decided to give compensation to the Japanese who were resettled in internment camps during WWII.

46. Politician: I know that some of you are concerned about my little run-in with the law. But I can assure you that my record speaks for itself.

47. **Blondes aren't dumb—they're just slow**

    Berlin—Blonde women are not dumber than brunettes or redheads, a reassuring study shows—they are just slower at processing information, take longer to react to stimuli and tend to retain less information for a shorter period of time than other women.

    "This should put an end to the insulting view that blondes are airheads," said Dr. Andrea Stenner, a blonde sociologist who studied more than 3,000 women for her doctoral research project.

    Weekly World News, October 15, 1996

48. (Pat Buchanan is a U.S. politician who advocates restricting immigration and ending welfare. During his campaign for the presidency in 1996 the following was said.)
    Pat Buchanan's speeches are better in the original German.

49. **One injured in one-car rollover**

    A West Valley, Utah, woman was injured Sunday when she apparently fell asleep at the wheel on Interstate 15.

    Utah Highway Patrol dispatch reports that 18-year-old Jennifer Gustin was heading north on I-15 Sunday morning about 7:30 a.m. when she fell asleep at the wheel.

    Gustin drifted off to the right and then over-corrected to the left. The vehicle rolled and then came to rest on its top in the median. Gustin was not wearing a seat belt and was partially ejected from the vehicle.

    UHP reports state she suffered from internal injuries.

    She was taken to Valley View Medical Center in Cedar City following the accident and was later transferred to Pioneer Valley hospital in West Valley, Utah.

    Nancy Camarena, 19, also of West Valley, was in the car, but received no injuries despite not wearing a seat belt.

    Tyson Hiatt, *The Spectrum,* April 30, 1996

50. On the day that Wislawa Symborski was awarded the Nobel Prize for Literature, there were orders for 12,000 copies of her most recent book. The publicist for her American publisher, Harcourt Brace, Dori Weintraub, said, "For a Polish poet, that's not bad."

51. (Advertisement)

If you love eggs, you'll love this news.

New studies say eggs are okay.

If you haven't heard the news, allow us to break it to you.

If you have normal cholesterol, follow a low-fat diet and love eggs, go ahead and enjoy them. Your cholesterol probably won't go up enough to notice.

Two recent studies published in a leading scientific journal showed that 20 healthy young men and 13 healthy young women with normal blood cholesterol levels could eat up to two eggs a day while on a low-fat diet without significantly boosting their blood cholesterol levels. Up to two eggs a day!

Research also shows that the amount of cholesterol consumed by the average American (300 mg to 400 mg a day) <u>does not</u> significantly boost blood cholesterol levels in most healthy people.

And how about this news?

Over the past 25 years, 227 studies conducted among 23,686 participants concluded that for most healthy people <u>saturated fat influences blood cholesterol levels more than dietary cholesterol.</u>

So tomorrow morning, whip up a couple of eggs and dig in. After all, with news this good, you're going to be real hungry.

Of course, not all the experts agree. So ask your doctor or a registered dietician about the best way to include eggs in your diet. One large egg has 215 mg of cholesterol and 1.5 grams of saturated fat (4.5 grams of total fat). An egg is also an inexpensive source of high-quality protein.

To find out more information about eggs, cholesterol and other topical issues, send for our free booklet, "Eggs and Good Health." Mail a stamped, self-addressed envelope to: American Egg Board, . . .

52. Conscious experience is a widespread phenomenon. It occurs at many levels of animal life, though we cannot be sure of its presence in the simpler organisms, and it is very difficult to say in general what provides evidence for it. (Some extremists have been prepared to deny it even of mammals other than man.) No doubt it occurs in countless forms totally unimaginable to us, on other planets in other solar systems throughout the universe. But no matter how the form may vary, the fact that an organism has conscious experience *at all* means, basically, that there is something it is like to *be* that organism. There may be further implications about the form of the experience; there may even (though I doubt it) be implications about the behavior of the organism. But fundamentally an organism has conscious states if and only if there is something that it is like to *be* that organism—something it is like *for* the organism.

Thomas Nagel, "What Is It to Be a Bat?"

53. Put a line through every slanter in the following, either eliminating it or rewriting neutrally. Then evaluate the argument.

Letter to the editor:

I am writing this letter to complain about the stupid, ridiculous $4 fee they are trying to impose on people using Snow Canyon [a large state park recreational area near St. George where there had previously been no fee]. It is getting harder and harder to find forms of recreation that don't cost money in this area. Now you have to pay $4, even if it's just to sit on the sand for a few minutes and collect some rays.

I've never really had a problem paying $5 to get into Zion's Park [a national park nearby], because going to Zion is an all day event. However, going to Snow Canyon is not. It's a place you go to after work or school when you only have a couple of free hours and a case of spring fever. Being charged for it would be comparable to charging $4 to enter the city park.

I don't feel that my presence in Snow Canyon is costing the state any extra expense that needs to be covered. The only facility I ever use is the road that goes through the park. It is my understanding that the fee isn't new, but they haven't had the staff to collect it until now. So in other words, they need the $4 to pay for the bigger staff, and the reason they need a bigger staff is to collect the $4 (a slight case of circular logic).

It just seems like we are losing more and more freedom all the time. Next they'll probably start charging us $4 to go on to the Sugar Loaf on the red hill. Who knows, maybe some day they will have government officials waiting on the streets to collect money from us every time we leave the house–to pay for the air we breathe–or has that already happened?

Shawn Williams, *The Spectrum,* March 24, 1996

54. Bring to class a letter to the editor. Read it to the class. Then read it with all the slanters replaced with neutral language.

10 Too Much Emotion

Key Words

appeal to pity   calling in your debts
appeal to fear   feel-good argument
scare tactics   apple polishing
appeal to spite   wishful thinking
two wrongs make a right

Exercises for Chapter 10

1. Write a *bad* argument in favor of affirmative action that is only an appeal to pity.

2. Find an advertisement that uses apple polishing.

3. Find an advertisement that uses an appeal to fear.

4. How would you classify an appeal to common practice among the types of arguments in this chapter?

5. Make up an appeal to some emotion for the next time a traffic officer stops you.

6. Report to the class on a "calling in your debts" argument you've heard.

7. Give an example of an appeal to spite that invokes what someone believes.

8. Define and give an example of an *appeal to patriotism*.
    (Samuel Johnson: "Patriotism is the last refuge of a scoundrel.")

9. Define and give an example of an *appeal to guilt*.

10. The opposite of an appeal to fear is an *appeal to bribery*. Define it and give an example.

For each of the following, decide if it is an argument. If it's an argument and fits one of the categories of this chapter, state the generic premise. Then say if it's a bad argument.

11. Zoe: We should stop all experimentation on animals right now. Imagine, hurting those poor doggies.

    Dick: But there's no reason why we shouldn't continue experimenting with cats. You know how they make me sneeze.

12. Before you buy that Japanese car, ask whether you want to see some Japanese tycoon get rich at your expense, or whether you'd prefer to see an American kid get a meal on his plate next week.

13. Vote for Harry. He knows how important your concerns are.

14. Dear Dr. E,
    I was very disappointed with my grade in your critical thinking course, but I'm sure that it was just a mistake in calculating my marks. Can I speak with you this Tuesday, right before I have lunch with my uncle, Dr. Jones, the Dean of Liberal Arts, where we plan to discuss sexual harassment on this campus?

    Sincerely, *Wanda Burnstile*

15. Go ahead. Live with your girlfriend. Who am I to say "No"? I'm just your mother. Break my heart.

16. Sunbathing does not cause skin cancer. If it did, how could I enjoy the beach?

17. Democracy is the best form of government, for otherwise this wouldn't be the greatest country in the world.

18. Smoking can't cause cancer or I would have been dead a long time ago.

19. (Advertisement)
    Impotent? You're not alone.
    Men naturally feel embarrassed about any sexual problem, but the fact is, impotence is a treatable medical symptom. Virtually every one of the twenty million men in America struggling with this problem could overcome it with the proper treatment from our physician, David Owensby, MD, The Diagnostic Center for Men in Las Vegas. We offer:

    –Medically effective, nonsurgical treatment in over 95% of all men.
    –Trained and certified male physicians and staff.
    –Strictly confidential & personalized care.
    –Coverage by most private insurance and Medicare.
    –More than 25,000 successfully treated men nationwide.

    When men find out how effectively we treat impotence, their most frequent comment is, "If I would have known, I would have worked up the courage to call sooner."
    Call us. We can help.

20. Dear Senator:
Before you make up your mind on how to vote on the abortion bill, I'd like to remind you that those who support abortion rights usually have small families. A few years from now all my six children, and the many children of my friends, all of whom believe abortion is morally wrong, will be voting.

21. Out? Out? That can't be a strike. You're always picking on me.

22. You mean that after we flew you here to Florida, paid for your lodging, showed you a wonderful time, all for free, you aren't going to buy a lot from us?

23. You shouldn't vote for gun control. It'll just make it easier for violent criminals to take advantage of us.

24. I know this diet's going to work because I have to lose 20 pounds by the end of this month.

25. (In Dr. E's class, if a student has to miss an exam, then he or she has to petition to be excused. If the petition is granted for a midterm, then the final counts that much more. If the petition is denied, the student fails the exam. Here's an excuse petition from one of his students, written before the exam. Is it a good argument? Should Dr. E grant the petition?)

October seventeenth through the twenty-first I will be out of town due to a family function. I am aware that my philosophy midterm falls on the seventeenth and, unfortunately, my flight leaves at 7 a.m. that morning. I am asking to please be excused from the midterm.

My boyfriend of two and a half years is standing as the best man in his brother's wedding. Being together for two years, I have become as much a part of his family as he is. This wedding is a once in a lifetime event and I want to be there to share it with him.

I am a 100% devoted student and would never intentionally miss an exam. However, this is something beyond my control. I understand that if my request is granted I will have to put forth extra effort and prepare myself for the final. With the only other alternative being to drop the course, I am fully prepared to do whatever it takes.

I have attached a copy of my flight reservation as well as a copy of the wedding invitation for verification. I am aware that many teachers would not even give me the opportunity to petition to be excused when the midterm is the case, but I would more than appreciate it if you would grant my request.

11   Fallacies

A summary of bad arguments

Key Words

    fallacy   generic premise
    structural fallacy   violating the rules of
    content fallacy   rational discussion

Exercises for Chapter 11

1.   What is a good argument?

2.   What are the three tests an argument must pass for it to be classified as good?

3.   State the Principle of Rational Discussion.

4. State the Guide to Repairing Arguments.

5. State the conditions under which an argument is unrepairable.

6. Is every valid or strong argument with true premises good? Explanation and/or counterexample.

7. If a very strong argument has twelve true premises and one dubious one, should we accept the conclusion?

8. What does a bad argument tell us about its conclusion?

9. What is our most reliable source of information about the world?

10. Why isn't a slippery slope argument classified as a structural fallacy?

11. Why isn't a false dilemma classified as a structural fallacy?

12. What is the generic premise for a common practice argument?

13. What is the generic premise for an appeal to common belief?

14. How can you distinguish between ridicule and an attempt to reduce to the absurd?

15. a.   Give an example of affirming the consequent.

    b.   What is the valid form of arguing that is similar?

16. a.   Give an example of denying the antecedent.

    b.   What is the valid form of arguing that is similar?

17. a.   Give an example of arguing backwards with "all."

    b.   What is the valid form of arguing that is similar?

18. a.   Give an example of arguing backwards with "almost all."

    b.   What is the strong form of arguing that is similar?

19. Give an example of reasoning in a chain with "some." Is it valid?

20. a. Give an example of arguing backwards with "no."

    b. What is the valid form of arguing that is similar?

21. Give an example of confusing objective and subjective. Is it a bad argument?

22. Give an example of drawing the line. Is it a bad argument?

23. Give an example of mistaking the person for the argument. Is it a bad argument?

24. Give an example of mistaking the person for the claim. Is it a bad argument?

25. Give an example of an appeal to authority that is not a bad argument.

26. Give an example of a phony refutation. Is it a bad argument?

27. Give an example of a false dilemma. Is it a bad argument?

28. Give an example of a slippery slope. Is it a bad argument?

29. Give an example of an appeal to pity. Is it a bad argument?

30. Give an example of an appeal to spite. Is it a bad argument?

31. Give an example of an appeal to fear. Is it a bad argument?

32. Give an example of a feel-good argument. Is it a bad argument?

33. Give an example of an argument that uses the generic premise of one of the types of content fallacies but which is not a bad argument.

34. Give an example of an argument that falls into more than one category of fallacy.

35. Give an example of begging the question. Is it a bad argument?

36. Give an example of an argument that someone might criticize as having an irrelevant premise or premises.

37. What's a strawman? Give an example.

38. Why are slanters included in the discussion of fallacies?

Writing Lesson 12

Here is your chance to show that you have all the basic skills to write an argument. Compose an argument either for or against the following:

"Cats should be legally prohibited from roaming freely in cities."

Check whether your instructor has chosen a *DIFFERENT TOPIC* for this assignment.

This time, write only a (maximum) one-page argument. It should be clear and well structured, since you will have written out the premises and conclusion for yourself first. You can recognize slanters and fallacies, so don't use any in your argument. And you know to include possible objections to your argument.

By now you should have learned a lot about writing arguments. You don't need more examples, just practice using the new ideas presented in the chapters. You can use as a guide Composing Good Arguments (p. 339 of the text), which summarizes many of the lessons you've learned.

Arguments for Analysis

Here's your chance to put together all you've learned in analyzing arguments. But first let's see how Tom is doing.

I'm not going to vote, because no matter who is president I still won't get a job.

Argument? (yes or no) Yes.

Conclusion (if unstated, add it): I shouldn't vote.

Premises: No matter who is president I still won't get a job.

Additional premises needed (if none, say so): Either I get a job when a new president is elected, or I shouldn't vote.

Classify (with the additional premises): <u>valid</u>   very strong ——————— weak

Good argument? (yes or no, with an explanation—possibly just the name of a fallacy)
    No. It's kind of a false dilemma. I think there was an exercise where it was called a perfectionist fallacy.

Excellent!

I hear that Brigitte Bardot is campaigning for animal rights. Isn't she the one who used to do advertisements for fur coats?

Argument? (yes or no) Yes—when rewritten.   *Good*

Conclusion (if unstated, add it): You shouldn't listen to Brigitte Bardot about animal rights.

Premises: Brigitte Bardot used to do advertisements for fur coats. (rewriting)

Additional premises needed (if none, say so): Don't listen to anything Brigitte Bardot says about fur coats.

Classify (with the additional premises):   valid   very strong ———————X– weak

Good argument? (yes or no, with an explanation—possibly just the name of a fallacy)
    No. I think it's mistaking the person for the argument.

At least you spotted that something was wrong. But you've forgotten that the only reason to add a premise is to make an argument valid or strong. The premise you added was just restating the conclusion. That would have made it valid, all right, but also would have been begging the question.

This is an example of a phony refutation. The premises that are needed are: "Brigitte Bardot doesn't believe the conclusion of her own arguments about animal rights if she was in ads for fur coats" and "If Brigitte Bardot doesn't believe the conclusion of her own argument, her argument is bad." Those will make the argument valid, but are clearly false.

—**Kelly is a moron.**
—**Why do you say that?**
—**Because she's so stupid**
Argument? (yes or no) Yes.
Conclusion (if unstated, add it):
Premises:
Additional premises needed (if none, say so):
Classify (with the additional premises):   valid   very strong —————X— weak
Good argument? (yes or no, with an explanation—possibly just the name of a fallacy)
This is just begging the question and a bad argument. Do I really need to fill in all
the blanks in your form when it's this obvious?

> *No, you don't need to fill in all the steps. As long as you're sure you've got it right. And
> you do—except that this begging the question is <u>valid</u>. You've confused "bad argument"
> with "weak argument."*

**Wash your car? Sure, and the next thing you know you'll want me to vacuum
the upholstery, and fill up the gas tank, and maybe even make a car payment
for you.**
Argument? (yes or no) Yes.
Conclusion (if unstated, add it): I shouldn't wash your car for you.
Premises:
Additional premises needed (if none, say so):
Classify (with the additional premises):   valid   very strong —————X— weak
Good argument? (yes or no, with an explanation—possibly just the name of a fallacy)
> This is a bad argument. I could rewrite it as a slippery slope, but it's pretty clear that
> the premises aren't plausible. It really borders on ridicule.
>
> *Good.*

For Exercises 1–64, fill in after the italics.

1. Smoking must be O.K. All my parents' friends do it, and the guys I hang out with all
    smoke.
    Argument? (yes or no)
    Conclusion (if unstated, add it):
    Premises:

    Additional premises needed (if none, say so):

    Classify (with the additional premises):   valid   very strong ————— weak
    Good argument? (yes or no, with an explanation—possibly just the name of a fallacy)

2. Mom: Well, what do you think? Did man evolve from cells and apes, or did God
         create man?

Dick: I don't know.
Mom: C'mon. You've got to have thought about it.
Dick: Oh, I guess I have, just never very hard. Beats me.
Mom: You've got to believe one side or the other. Which is it?

Argument? (yes or no)
Conclusion (if unstated, add it):
Premises:

Additional premises needed (if none, say so):

Classify (with the additional premises):   valid   very strong ——————— weak
Good argument? (yes or no, with an explanation—possibly just the name of a fallacy)

3. How can you not believe in God? Could your parents, friends, your family all be wrong?
Argument? (yes or no)
Conclusion (if unstated, add it):
Premises:

Additional premises needed (if none, say so):

Classify (with the additional premises):   valid   very strong ——————— weak
Good argument? (yes or no, with an explanation—possibly just the name of a fallacy)

4.

Argument? (yes or no)
Conclusion (if unstated, add it):
Premises:

Additional premises needed (if none, say so):

Classify (with the additional premises):   valid   very strong ——————— weak
Good argument? (yes or no, with an explanation—possibly just the name of a fallacy)

5. My opponent says he is against tightening the immigration laws and posting more guards along the Mexican border. That's easy for him to say, living in an expensive home in San Francisco.

   Argument? (yes or no)
   Conclusion (if unstated, add it):
   Premises:

   Additional premises needed (if none, say so):

   Classify (with the additional premises):   valid   very strong ——————— weak
   Good argument? (yes or no, with an explanation—possibly just the name of a fallacy)

6. Dan was clever but he couldn't go to college. His father disappeared leaving a lot of debt, and his mother was terminally ill. So Dan had to take care of his mother and work full-time.

   Argument? (yes or no)
   Conclusion (if unstated, add it):
   Premises:

   Additional premises needed (if none, say so):

   Classify (with the additional premises):   valid   very strong ——————— weak
   Good argument? (yes or no, with an explanation—possibly just the name of a fallacy)

7. Fingerprinting may intimidate crooks, but businesses don't want to scare off law-abiding customers, too. So they're trying to put a positive spin on a procedure long used mainly on criminals.

   When customers at Food Lion supermarkets object to the "Authentiprint" program, cashiers are instructed to say, "It's for your own protection."

   Even the word "fingerprint" is taboo in some circles. The preferred terms are "finger image" or "finger minutiae."

   When MasterCard International Inc. announced last year it was considering the use of biometrics for identifying cardholders, it took pains to explain that when customers pressed their dye-coated fingertip against a card, they shouldn't consider that being fingerprinted.

   "One of the most important factors to be aware of with finger minutiae is that we are not talking about fingerprinting," a company news release quoted senior Vice President Joel S. Lisker as saying.

   Associated Press, July 13, 1997

   Argument? (yes or no)
   Conclusion (if unstated, add it):

Premises:

Additional premises needed (if none, say so):

Classify (with the additional premises):   valid   very strong ——————— weak

Good argument? (yes or no, with an explanation—possibly just the name of a fallacy)

8. Stop mowing my lawn in the morning? Just because you want to sleep? Next thing you know you'll want me to stop playing my radio. And not leave my car running in the driveway.

Argument? (yes or no)
Conclusion (if unstated, add it):
Premises:

Additional premises needed (if none, say so):

Classify (with the additional premises):   valid   very strong ——————— weak

Good argument? (yes or no, with an explanation—possibly just the name of a fallacy)

9. —I know that there is ESP.
    —How?
    —If there weren't, there'd be too much left unexplained.

Argument? (yes or no)
Conclusion (if unstated, add it):
Premises:

Additional premises needed (if none, say so):

Classify (with the additional premises):   valid   very strong ——————— weak

Good argument? (yes or no, with an explanation—possibly just the name of a fallacy)

10. She looks asleep. But she's not been breathing for over an hour and her body is very cold. Even if I tickle her, she doesn't move. When a person is not breathing, the body is cold and doesn't move, the person is dead. So she is dead.

Argument? (yes or no)
Conclusion (if unstated, add it):

Premises:

Additional premises needed (if none, say so):

Classify (with the additional premises): valid   very strong ——————— weak
Good argument? (yes or no, with an explanation—possibly just the name of a fallacy)

11. Parking is still difficult on campus. They said they'd build a parking garage, but that'll take ages. They should get rid of the fees they started charging us for parking on campus.
    Argument? (yes or no)
    Conclusion (if unstated, add it):
    Premises:

    Additional premises needed (if none, say so):

    Classify (with the additional premises): valid   very strong ——————— weak
    Good argument? (yes or no, with an explanation—possibly just the name of a fallacy)

12. Unprotected sex is O.K. I know lots of people who do it, and what's the worst that can happen? You get pregnant.
    Argument? (yes or no)
    Conclusion (if unstated, add it):
    Premises:

    Additional premises needed (if none, say so):

    Classify (with the additional premises): valid   very strong ——————— weak
    Good argument? (yes or no, with an explanation—possibly just the name of a fallacy)

13. Psychiatrist: You are suffering from delusions of grandeur.
    Dr. E: What? What? There's nothing wrong with me.
    Psychiatrist: It is not normal to think that you are the smartest man in the world.
    Dr. E: But I am.
    Psychiatrist: Certainly *you* think so.
    Dr. E: Look, if Arnold Schwarzenegger came in and said he was the strongest man in the world, would you think he's crazy?

Psychiatrist: Crazy? I did not say you were crazy. You are suffering from delusions of grandeur.

Dr. E: O.K. Would Arnold Schwarzenegger be suffering from delusions of grandeur?

Psychiatrist: Possibly not.

Dr. E: So someone has to be the smartest person in the world.

Psychiatrist: That's true.

Dr. E: Why not me?

Psychiatrist: Because you are not.

Dr. E: How do you know?

Psychiatrist: Trust me.

Dr. E: You can't even define "delusions of grandeur," can you?

Psychiatrist: I am trained to spot it when it occurs.

Argument? (yes or no)

Conclusion (if unstated, add it):

Premises:

Additional premises needed (if none, say so):

Classify (with the additional premises):   valid   very strong ———————— weak

Good argument? (yes or no, with an explanation—possibly just the name of a fallacy)

14. Usually grocery stores have salt. I haven't been to Von's grocery, but they must have salt, too.

Argument? (yes or no)

Conclusion (if unstated, add it):

Premises:

Additional premises needed (if none, say so):

Classify (with the additional premises):   valid   very strong ———————— weak

Good argument? (yes or no, with an explanation—possibly just the name of a fallacy)

15. [After a chemical explosion at a plant, a man was interviewed who worked in the section where one man was killed by the explosion and four were injured. He had been on vacation at the time.]

Powell said the idea of working every day in a plant filled with toxic chemicals hasn't worried him, and he plans to return when his vacation is over.

"There are toxic chemicals in your house under your sink," he said. "There is constant training on how to handle them, and if you follow those guidelines, you're OK. Every job has a potential hazard."

Tyson Hiatt, in *The Spectrum,* July 31, 1997

Argument? (yes or no)

Conclusion (if unstated, add it):

Premises:

Additional premises needed (if none, say so):

Classify (with the additional premises):   valid   very strong ———————— weak

Good argument? (yes or no, with an explanation—possibly just the name of a fallacy)

16. Tom: Everyone I know who's taken the critical thinking course has really enjoyed and profited from it.

    Harry: Suzy took that course, so she enjoyed it, too?

Argument? (yes or no)

Conclusion (if unstated, add it):

Premises:

Additional premises needed (if none, say so):

Classify (with the additional premises):   valid   very strong ———————— weak

Good argument? (yes or no, with an explanation—possibly just the name of a fallacy)

17. Tom: Everyone in the U.S. should have to speak English. Everyone's got to talk the same, so we can communicate, and it'll unify the country.

    Lee: Sure. But I have real trouble understanding people from New York. So why not make everyone speak just like you, with a midwestern accent?

Argument? (yes or no)

Conclusion (if unstated, add it):

Premises:

Additional premises needed (if none, say so):

Classify (with the additional premises):   valid   very strong ———————— weak

Good argument? (yes or no, with an explanation—possibly just the name of a fallacy)

18. Zoe: Here in the newspaper it says that some of those fraternity guys were crazy
enough to swallow goldfish.

Dick: Stands to reason. Lots of football players are in the fraternities, and they're wild.

Argument? (yes or no)

Conclusion (if unstated, add it):

Premises:

Additional premises needed (if none, say so):

Classify (with the additional premises):   valid   very strong ——————— weak

Good argument? (yes or no, with an explanation—possibly just the name of a fallacy)

19. (Summarizing a discussion heard on National Public Radio)

An experiment is being conducted to study temperature changes in the ocean using very
low frequency sound waves that will be generated in the South Pacific and picked up
near the Arctic Circle. The sound waves will be generated 2 times per day for 10 years.

The interviewer, speaking to one of the people involved in the experiment, said
that perhaps we shouldn't do this, since we don't know the effect of the sound on
whales. The experimenter replied that the ocean is already so full of sound, if you count
all the acousticians vs. all the supertankers, the supertankers would win hands down.

Argument? (yes or no)

Conclusion (if unstated, add it):

Premises:

Additional premises needed (if none, say so):

Classify (with the additional premises):   valid   very strong ——————— weak

Good argument? (yes or no, with an explanation—possibly just the name of a fallacy)

20. Reggie: Look, I deserve at least a C in this course. By your own standards I earned
a C. Here, I did all my homework and contributed in class, just like you said.
I know I only got a D+ on the final, but our other work was supposed to be
able to outweigh that.

Dr. E: Perhaps I did say that, but I can't go back and change your grade. I'd have to change a lot of grades.

Reggie: That's unfair and unethical. I'll take it to the chairman.

Later in the chairman's office

Dr. E: So this student is going to come in and see you to complain about his grade. He thinks that just because he showed up regularly and handed in some homework he should pass the course.

Argument? (yes or no)
Conclusion (if unstated, add it):
Premises:

Additional premises needed (if none, say so):

Classify (with the additional premises):   valid   very strong ———————— weak
Good argument? (yes or no, with an explanation—possibly just the name of a fallacy)

21. Tom: Suzy said that Chapter 6 won't be on the final.

    Harry: You'd believe that ditsy cheerleader?

Argument? (yes or no)
Conclusion (if unstated, add it):
Premises:

Additional premises needed (if none, say so):

Classify (with the additional premises):   valid   very strong ——————— weak
Good argument? (yes or no, with an explanation—possibly just the name of a fallacy)

22. Fred is a doctor who has been working in this hospital as a chief of surgery for 10 years. So he graduated from medical school.

Argument? (yes or no)
Conclusion (if unstated, add it):
Premises:

Additional premises needed (if none, say so):

Classify (with the additional premises):   valid   very strong ——————— weak
Good argument? (yes or no, with an explanation—possibly just the name of a fallacy)

23. Chris finds most women with dark hair more attractive than women with light hair. Marissa has dark hair and Erika has light hair. Therefore, Chris finds Marissa more attractive.

Argument? (yes or no)
Conclusion (if unstated, add it):
Premises:

Additional premises needed (if none, say so):

Classify (with the additional premises):   valid   very strong ——————— weak
Good argument? (yes or no, with an explanation—possibly just the name of a fallacy)

24. There's only one way to stop Las Vegas from being choked on smog and traffic, and that's to stop migration to the city by limiting the number of building permits.

Argument? (yes or no)
Conclusion (if unstated, add it):
Premises:

Additional premises needed (if none, say so):

Classify (with the additional premises):   valid   very strong ————— weak
Good argument? (yes or no, with an explanation—possibly just the name of a fallacy)

25. I read that the county wants to start registering dogs. We've got to resist it. The next thing you know they'll make owning a dog illegal.

Argument? (yes or no)
Conclusion (if unstated, add it):
Premises:

Additional premises needed (if none, say so):

Classify (with the additional premises):   valid   very strong ————— weak
Good argument? (yes or no, with an explanation—possibly just the name of a fallacy)

26. Ms. Fletcher is a good teacher. She gives great parties.

Argument? (yes or no)
Conclusion (if unstated, add it):

Premises:

Additional premises needed (if none, say so):

Classify (with the additional premises):   valid   very strong ——————— weak
Good argument? (yes or no, with an explanation—possibly just the name of a fallacy)

27. The incumbent is going to win the election. She's way ahead in the opinion polls, and the opinion polls are seldom wrong.

Argument? (yes or no)
Conclusion (if unstated, add it):
Premises:

Additional premises needed (if none, say so):

Classify (with the additional premises):   valid   very strong ——————— weak
Good argument? (yes or no, with an explanation—possibly just the name of a fallacy)

28. Tom: Everyone I know who's passed the critical thinking course has really enjoyed and profited from it.
    Harry: Suzy enjoyed that course.
    Dick: So she must have passed it. Amazing.

Argument? (yes or no)
Conclusion (if unstated, add it):
Premises:

Additional premises needed (if none, say so):

Classify (with the additional premises):   valid   very strong ——————— weak
Good argument? (yes or no, with an explanation—possibly just the name of a fallacy)

29. Raise tuition? That's wrong. It's already so expensive to go to school, what with the cost of books, and food, and rent. It's really wrong to raise tuition.

Argument? (yes or no)

Conclusion (if unstated, add it):
Premises:

Additional premises needed (if none, say so):

Classify (with the additional premises):   valid   very strong ——————— weak
Good argument? (yes or no, with an explanation—possibly just the name of a fallacy)

30. You say you want to raise tuition again? Why not raise the parking fees, too? And the dorm contracts. And raise prices at the cafeteria, while you're at it. Or maybe even charge students for using the library. You could balance the university's budget for sure that way.

Argument? (yes or no)
Conclusion (if unstated, add it):
Premises:

Additional premises needed (if none, say so):

Classify (with the additional premises):   valid   very strong ————— weak
Good argument? (yes or no, with an explanation—possibly just the name of a fallacy)

31. You shouldn't keep a gun in the house. If an intruder breaks in, it could be used against you.

Argument? (yes or no)
Conclusion (if unstated, add it):
Premises:

Additional premises needed (if none, say so):

Classify (with the additional premises):   valid   very strong ————— weak
Good argument? (yes or no, with an explanation—possibly just the name of a fallacy)

32. You should take your cousin to the dance because she's shy, and doesn't go out much, and is really sad since her cat died. It would make her feel good.

Argument? (yes or no)
Conclusion (if unstated, add it):
Premises:

Additional premises needed (if none, say so):

Classify (with the additional premises): valid   very strong ——————— weak
Good argument? (yes or no, with an explanation—possibly just the name of a fallacy)

33. The U. S. Attorney General said that there was no need to investigate the president's campaign financing. So the president didn't do anything wrong.

Argument? (yes or no)
Conclusion (if unstated, add it):
Premises:

Additional premises needed (if none, say so):

Classify (with the additional premises): valid   very strong ——————— weak
Good argument? (yes or no, with an explanation—possibly just the name of a fallacy)

34. I've got to get new clothes, Mom. You don't want me to look like a slob, do you?

Argument? (yes or no)
Conclusion (if unstated, add it):
Premises:

Additional premises needed (if none, say so):

Classify (with the additional premises): valid   very strong ——————— weak
Good argument? (yes or no, with an explanation—possibly just the name of a fallacy)

35. Rice is good for you. A billion Chinese can't be wrong.

Argument? (yes or no)
Conclusion (if unstated, add it):
Premises:

Additional premises needed (if none, say so):

Classify (with the additional premises):   valid   very strong ————————— weak

Good argument? (yes or no, with an explanation—possibly just the name of a fallacy)

36. Dick: If Suzy doesn't pass her critical thinking class, she can't be a cheerleader unless she goes to summer school.

    Zoe: She's going to fail that course for sure.

    Dick: Looks like she'll be going to summer school.

    Argument? (yes or no)
    Conclusion (if unstated, add it):
    Premises:

    Additional premises needed (if none, say so):

    Classify (with the additional premises):   valid   very strong ————————— weak

    Good argument? (yes or no, with an explanation—possibly just the name of a fallacy)

37. Of course the Mayor is arguing against limiting the number of building permits. He's got his own real estate office.

    Argument? (yes or no)
    Conclusion (if unstated, add it):
    Premises:

    Additional premises needed (if none, say so):

    Classify (with the additional premises):   valid   very strong ————————— weak

    Good argument? (yes or no, with an explanation—possibly just the name of a fallacy)

38. Dick: Very few of the cheerleaders fail courses. They're too motivated.

    Lee: Suzy's a cheerleader. So she passes all her courses. Hmmm.

    Argument? (yes or no)
    Conclusion (if unstated, add it):
    Premises:

    Additional premises needed (if none, say so):

Classify (with the additional premises):   valid   very strong ——————— weak

    Good argument? (yes or no, with an explanation—possibly just the name of a fallacy)

39. Letter to the editor:

Governor Pete Wilson signed a law making California the first state to require chemical castration of repeat child molesters. . . .   This is one law that should be enacted in every state in the United States. I see the American Civil Liberties Union has called this procedure barbaric. However, the ACLU doesn't consider how barbaric it is when an adult molests a child.

                                       Roger E. Nielsen, *The Salt Lake Tribune,* October 6, 1996

Argument? (yes or no)

Conclusion (if unstated, add it):

Premises:

Additional premises needed (if none, say so):

Classify (with the additional premises):   valid   very strong ——————— weak

Good argument? (yes or no, with an explanation—possibly just the name of a fallacy)

40. I'm going to give up smoking because I read that the Surgeon General says it's bad for your health.

Argument? (yes or no)

Conclusion (if unstated, add it):

Premises:

Additional premises needed (if none, say so):

Classify (with the additional premises):   valid   very strong ——————— weak

Good argument? (yes or no, with an explanation—possibly just the name of a fallacy)

41. I'm now in favor of allowing abortions, since the Surgeon General said that it should be legal.

Argument? (yes or no)

Conclusion (if unstated, add it):

Premises:

Additional premises needed (if none, say so):

Classify (with the additional premises):   valid   very strong ——————— weak
Good argument? (yes or no, with an explanation—possibly just the name of a fallacy)

42. —Our kids should be allowed to pray in schools.
    —What? If they're not allowed to pray, maybe God won't exist?

Argument? (yes or no)
Conclusion (if unstated, add it):
Premises:

Additional premises needed (if none, say so):

Classify (with the additional premises):   valid   very strong ——————— weak
Good argument? (yes or no, with an explanation—possibly just the name of a fallacy)

43. Maria: Dr. E's course is just great.
    Suzy: It's easy for you to say—you just got an A on the midterm.

Argument? (yes or no)
Conclusion (if unstated, add it):
Premises:

Additional premises needed (if none, say so):

Classify (with the additional premises):   valid   very strong ——————— weak
Good argument? (yes or no, with an explanation—possibly just the name of a fallacy)

44. Suzy: Either Dr. E doesn't like me or he misgraded my test, because I got a D.

Argument? (yes or no)
Conclusion (if unstated, add it):
Premises:

Additional premises needed (if none, say so):

Classify (with the additional premises):   valid   very strong ——————— weak
Good argument? (yes or no, with an explanation—possibly just the name of a fallacy)

45. Zoe: If you don't stop sleeping around you're going to catch a venereal disease.
    Suzy: That's just your opinion.

Argument? (yes or no)
Conclusion (if unstated, add it):
Premises:

Additional premises needed (if none, say so):

Classify (with the additional premises): valid   very strong —————— weak
Good argument? (yes or no, with an explanation—possibly just the name of a fallacy)

46. Dick: I can't believe that *Failing in Atlanta* didn't win an Oscar.
Zoe: Nobody understands what art is.

Argument? (yes or no)
Conclusion (if unstated, add it):
Premises:

Additional premises needed (if none, say so):

Classify (with the additional premises): valid   very strong —————— weak
Good argument? (yes or no, with an explanation—possibly just the name of a fallacy)

47. Zoe: It's not healthy to eat a lot of cholesterol.
Dick: Why?
Zoe: Because it's not good for your body.

Argument? (yes or no)
Conclusion (if unstated, add it):
Premises:

Additional premises needed (if none, say so):

Classify (with the additional premises): valid   very strong —————— weak
Good argument? (yes or no, with an explanation—possibly just the name of a fallacy)

48. You say we should legalize drugs. So you want everyone running around doped up, kids whacked out, and everybody being unproductive members of society.

Argument? (yes or no)
Conclusion (if unstated, add it):
Premises:

Additional premises needed (if none, say so):

Classify (with the additional premises): valid   very strong ——————— weak
Good argument? (yes or no, with an explanation—possibly just the name of a fallacy)

49. Dick: If Freud was right, then the only things that matter to a man are fame, riches, and the love of beautiful women.

Zoe: But Ralph is poor, single, never married and uninterested in women (or men), and certainly not famous. Yet he's happy. So Freud was wrong.

Dick: Freud wasn't wrong. If we take into account the possibility of sublimation, we can see that Ralph is only happy because he has sublimated his desire for beautiful women into caring for his dogs. And he puts so much time into caring for his dogs because he hopes, unconsciously perhaps, to become famous as a great dog lover. And maybe rich, too. Though if you ask him, he'll say he's content.

Argument? (yes or no)
Conclusion (if unstated, add it):
Premises:

Additional premises needed (if none, say so):

Classify (with the additional premises): valid   very strong ——————— weak

Good argument? (yes or no, with an explanation—possibly just the name of a fallacy)

50.

Argument? (yes or no)
Conclusion (if unstated, add it): `

Premises:

Additional premises needed (if none, say so):

Classify (with the additional premises):   valid   very strong ——————— weak
Good argument? (yes or no, with an explanation—possibly just the name of a fallacy)

51. (Contributed by a student)

Student athletes should not be given special leniency in assigning course marks. Student athletes who do receive special leniency turn out to be failures. They are not given the mental challenge that regular students are given. All student athletes that I have ever met or seen that have received special leniency have not graduated from college. In order to make something of yourself, you must first graduate from college. Everyone that I have ever met or seen wants to make a good living and make something of themselves. On the other hand, all of the student athletes I know that do not receive special leniency have graduated and have been successful in life. Therefore, student athletes that want to be successful in life must not receive special leniency.

Argument? (yes or no)
Conclusion (if unstated, add it):
Premises:

Additional premises needed (if none, say so):

Classify (with the additional premises):   valid   very strong ——————— weak
Good argument? (yes or no, with an explanation—possibly just the name of a fallacy)

52. I resent that. Our company is not racist. We give a donation to the NAACP every year.

Argument? (yes or no)
Conclusion (if unstated, add it):
Premises:

Additional premises needed (if none, say so):

Classify (with the additional premises):   valid   very strong ——————— weak
Good argument? (yes or no, with an explanation—possibly just the name of a fallacy)

53. Professor Zzzyzzx: I am surprised you vas failing dat Suzy kid. She doesn't
    vork too hard, but I vasn't thinking she vas *so* bad.

    Dr. E: Maybe not. But she deserved to fail. When I joked that the first thing that goes
    when you get older is your memory . . . You know the one?

    Professor Zzzyzzx: Maybe, but, alas, mine memory is not so goot, now.

    Dr. E: So I say, "And the second thing, the second thing is . . ." Then I pause
    and usually everyone laughs.

    Professor Zzzyzzx: Jah, so? Is dat a goot joke?

    Dr. E: But Suzy said, "Your looks." No way she deserved to pass.

    Argument? (yes or no)
    Conclusion (if unstated, add it):
    Premises:

    Additional premises needed (if none, say so):

    Classify (with the additional premises):   valid   very strong ——————— weak
    Good argument? (yes or no, with an explanation—possibly just the name of a fallacy)

54. Lee: Every computer science major is a nerd.
    Maria: None of the cheerleaders are majoring in computer science.
    Lee: Right. So none of them are nerds.

    Argument? (yes or no)
    Conclusion (if unstated, add it):
    Premises:

    Additional premises needed (if none, say so):

    Classify (with the additional premises):   valid   very strong ——————— weak
    Good argument? (yes or no, with an explanation—possibly just the name of a fallacy)

55. We should not support Jerry's Kids. After all, many gay organizations try to get us to
    support that charity.

    Argument? (yes or no)
    Conclusion (if unstated, add it):
    Premises:

    Additional premises needed (if none, say so):

Classify (with the additional premises):   valid   very strong ——————— weak

Good argument? (yes or no, with an explanation—possibly just the name of a fallacy)

56. Suppose this patient really does have hepatitis. Well, anyone who has hepatitis will, after a week, begin to appear jaundiced. Yellowing of the eyeballs and skin will proceed dramatically after two weeks. So if he has hepatitis now, since he's been feeling sick for two weeks, he should be jaundiced. But he isn't. So he doesn't have hepatitis.

Argument? (yes or no)
Conclusion (if unstated, add it):
Premises:

Additional premises needed (if none, say so):

Classify (with the additional premises):   valid   very strong ——————— weak

Good argument? (yes or no, with an explanation—possibly just the name of a fallacy)

57. I've got three choices: I can major in accounting and spend my life behind dusty account ledgers and computers, or I can major in finance and spend all my time talking to stuffy bankers and hot-shot brokers, or I can drop out of school and become a waiter and earn $30,000 a year in Las Vegas. Those are the choices, since I'm too far along on a business major to change to another. I'd really prefer to be a nurse. But it's best to settle on being a waiter.

Argument? (yes or no)
Conclusion (if unstated, add it):
Premises:

Additional premises needed (if none, say so):

Classify (with the additional premises):   valid   very strong ——————— weak

Good argument? (yes or no, with an explanation—possibly just the name of a fallacy)

58. (Monday)   Zoe: If you eat that candy bar, then you'll gain weight.
    (Friday)   Dick: I gained weight this week.
               Zoe: So you ate that candy bar.

Argument? (yes or no)
Conclusion (if unstated, add it):
Premises:

Additional premises needed (if none, say so):

Classify (with the additional premises): valid   very strong ——————— weak

Good argument? (yes or no, with an explanation—possibly just the name of a fallacy)

59. Dick: I can't stand Siamese cats. Ugh. They all have those strange blue eyes.
Suzy: Mary Ellen's got a kitten with blue eyes. I didn't know it was Siamese.

Argument? (yes or no)
Conclusion (if unstated, add it):
Premises:

Additional premises needed (if none, say so):

Classify (with the additional premises): valid   very strong ——————— weak

Good argument? (yes or no, with an explanation—possibly just the name of a fallacy)

60. Zoe: If you don't start helping around the house, doing the dishes and cleaning up, then you don't really understand what it means to be a part of a couple.
Dick: O.K., O.K., look, I'm vacuuming. I'll do the dishes tonight.
Zoe: So you do understand what it means to be part of a couple.

Argument? (yes or no)
Conclusion (if unstated, add it):
Premises:

Additional premises needed (if none, say so):

Classify (with the additional premises): valid   very strong ——————— weak

Good argument? (yes or no, with an explanation—possibly just the name of a fallacy)

61. Zoe: I wear a size 7 blue jeans.
Dick: J.C. Penney's carries Levi's in all sizes.
Zoe: So I don't need to worry about finding my size when I go shopping at Penney's.

Argument? (yes or no)
Conclusion (if unstated, add it):

Premises:

Additional premises needed (if none, say so):

Classify (with the additional premises):   valid   very strong ——————— weak
Good argument? (yes or no, with an explanation—possibly just the name of a fallacy)

62. How can sunbathing be bad for you? Lying out in the sun is very relaxing. How can that be bad?

Argument? (yes or no)
Conclusion (if unstated, add it):
Premises:

Additional premises needed (if none, say so):

Classify (with the additional premises):   valid   very strong ——————— weak
Good argument? (yes or no, with an explanation—possibly just the name of a fallacy)

63. Suzy (to Tom): Will you work on an extra credit assignment with me? You're very articulate and have a wonderful grasp of the English language. I know we would get the assignment right if we worked on it together.

Argument? (yes or no)
Conclusion (if unstated, add it):
Premises:

Additional premises needed (if none, say so):

Classify (with the additional premises):   valid   very strong ——————— weak
Good argument? (yes or no, with an explanation—possibly just the name of a fallacy)

64. Tom: I can't believe you're an hour late!
    Suzy: What are you talking about?
    Tom: You said you'd meet me here at 7 to work on the English assignment.
    Suzy: I am not late.
    Tom: It's almost 8.
    Suzy: I said I'd be here a little after 7.

Argument? (yes or no)
Conclusion (if unstated, add it):
Premises:

Additional premises needed (if none, say so):

Classify (with the additional premises): valid   very strong ——————— weak
Good argument? (yes or no, with an explanation—possibly just the name of a fallacy)

Here are some longer arguments. You'll need to use everything you know to analyze these. Eliminate the slanters and pay attention to unstated premises. To give you an idea of what's involved, I've included a long exercise that Tom did.

Morass of value judgments

Well-intentioned DUI law chips away at individual rights.

When a new state law goes into effect today, police will be allowed to use "reasonable force" to obtain blood samples from first-time drunken driving suspects who refuse to take a breath test. *1*

Defense attorneys plan to challenge this law, citing the potential for unnecessary violence resulting from attempts to enforce it. *2* The law's proponents say it is necessary to obtain adequate evidence to lock up violators of drunken driving laws and force is already allowed against repeat offenders. *3* One supporter of the law was quoted on television recently saying that people who are suspected of driving drunk give up their rights. *4*

There is a hidden danger with laws that chip away at the Fourth Amendment prohibition against unreasonable searches and seizures. *5*

Yes, we need to vigorously fight drunken driving, take away driver's licenses of those who refuse breath tests, and lock up repeat offenders who are obviously impaired according to eyewitness testimony. *6* But our hard-won individual rights, freedoms and protections should not be flippantly squandered, even in the name of public safety. *7*

The danger is that once we begin to buy into the concept that the rights of society as a whole are superior to the rights of the individual, then we begin to slide into a morass of value judgments. *8* If it is more important for society to stop drunken driving than for the suspected driver to be free from unreasonable search of his blood veins and seizure of his blood, then might it not be argued that it is more important for elected officials and sports heroes to get organ transplants than mere working stiffs? *9*

If rights can be weighed against societal imperatives, what next? *10* Our rights against self incrimination? *11* Freedom of religion? *12* Speech? *13* Fair trial? *14* The vote? *15*

Having personally experienced the heavy hand of tyranny, the Founding Fathers wrote: "The right of the people to be secure in their persons, houses, papers, and effects, against unreasonable searches and seizures, shall not be violated, and no Warrants shall issue, but upon probable cause, supported by Oath or affirmation, and particularly describing the place to be searched, and the person or things to be seized." *16*

Rather than slug it out in the courts, we would hope that our various police forces would give a second thought or more before resorting to constitutionally questionable exercises. *17* What difference is there between a hypodermic needle and a battering ram? *18*

If we vigilantly guard and revere the rights of individuals, society in general will be better off. *19*

Editorial, *Las Vegas Review-Journal,* October 1, 1995

Conclusion: Police should not be allowed to use reasonable force to obtain blood samples from first-time drunken driving suspects who refuse to take a breath test.

Premises: 1. This is just stating the background. The editor uses a downplayer in putting quotes around "reasonable force." *It's not a downplayer. It's a quote. It might also show that he doesn't believe the words have a clear meaning.*

2. I suppose this is true. It shows that someone other than the editors think there's a problem. But so what?

3. Gives the other side. Counterargument.

4. Big deal. So one nut said that. Doesn't really contribute to the argument. He'd have to show that a lot of people thought that. Otherwise it's probably a strawman.

5. "Chip away" is a slanter. Dysphemism. Anyway, he hasn't shown that this law goes against the Fourth Amendment. Apparently the lawmakers didn't think so. If it does, it'll be declared unconstitutional, and that's that. Doesn't really help his conclusion. Waving the flag, sort of.

6. Sets out his position. Sort of a counterargument to the supporters of the bill. Shows he's not unreasonable. Giving a bit to the other side, I guess. Doesn't seem to help get to his conclusion.

7. "Hard-won" is there without proof. Perhaps it was hard-won. Possibly adds to the argument by adding a premise: "Whatever is hard-won should not be given up." But that's false. There'd never be peace treaties then without unconditional surrender. "Flippantly squandered" is a dysphemism, and he hasn't shown that they are flippantly squandered. But worst is that when he talks about rights, protections, etc. It's not clear what "right" he is talking about. If it's the one in the Fourth Amendment, he's got to prove that this law is giving that up, which he hasn't. Otherwise he's just waving the flag.

8. He's got to prove this. It's crucial to his argument.

9. This is supposedly support for 8, but it doesn't work. I think the answer is "No." He's got to show it's "Yes."

11.–15. These are rhetorical questions, too. As premises they seem very dubious. Altogether they're a slippery slope.

16. The first part is just there like "hard-won" was before. Quoting the Fourth Amendment doesn't make it clear to me that this law violates it.

17. "Slug it out in the courts" is a dysphemism. He hasn't shown that the law is constitutionally questionable.

18. Another rhetorical question with a stupid comparison. My answer is "Plenty." He's got to convince me that there's no difference. The old slippery slope again.

19. Vague and unproved. Can't be support for the conclusion, and it's not the conclusion, either. Does nothing.

It's a bad argument. Too many slanters, and there's really no support for the conclusion.

Very, very good. Only you need to expand on why it's a bad argument. What exactly are the claims that have any value in getting the conclusion?

All that 2 elicits is, "So?" We can't guess what's the missing premise that could save this support. He doesn't knock off 3 (perhaps 4 is intended to do that, sort of reducing to the absurd?). The support for 8 is a worthless slippery slope (9–15), plus some one person's comments that we'd have to take to be exemplary of lots of peoples (there's a missing premise: "If one person said this on television, then lots of people believe it," which is very dubious). Number 16 is crucial, but he hasn't shown that 7 follows from it. That's the heart of the argument that he's left out (as you noted): He's got to show that this law really violates the Fourth Amendment and, for 19, that it isn't a good trade-off of personal rights vs. society's rights. So there's really no support for his conclusion. That's why it's bad. <u>The use of slanters is bad, but it doesn't make the argument bad.</u> We can eliminate them and then see what's wrong. I'd give B+/A– for this. Incorporate this discussion in your presentation to the class and you'll get an A.

There's no set procedure for analyzing these arguments, though you can use the steps on page 170 of Chapter 7 as a guideline, and complete your assignment on separate pages.

65. *(Reputed to come from a Howard Stern show in April, 1996. They're discussing Howard Stern's investment in tobacco/cigarette industry stocks.)*

Caller: Howard, how can you invest in killing people?

Stern: What do you mean? I made a good business investment.

Caller: You invested in killing kids.

Stern: Listen buddy, there are laws that say you have to be eighteen to buy cigarettes. If store owners sell to underage kids, that's their own greedy fault; that's not my fault or the fault of the tobacco company.

Caller: But you invested in the tobacco company that lies to the government, and cigarettes kill.

Stern: What's this lie to the government? . . . I don't care–everybody lies–you lie. If someone is so stupid they want to smoke, that's their problem, we all know it's bad to smoke. That's why I don't smoke, I'm not stupid. But if someone else wants to smoke, that's his right, he has the right to be stupid, and I have the right to invest my money in a company that will make me money.

Caller: Howard, it's not right, next thing you know you'll be investing in AIDS.

Stern: You idiot, you can't invest in disease. I invested in a company. You don't know what you're talking about, get off my phone line you jerk. (Hangs up)

66. **St. George doesn't need a $30,000 a year mayor**
Letter to the editor:

The proposal by city officials to give themselves a generous raise has caused much concern among St. George residents, especially the ones who are barely getting by on the notoriously low salaries paid in Dixie [the southwest corner of Utah].

Even if Dan McArthur were to become a full-time mayor, how could he justify $30,000 a year? Since City Manager Gary Esplin is "handling everything from budgets and water treatment to planning and zoning disputes," why do we even need a mayor? And where would St. George find the money to give the proposed salary increases precedence over more critical municipal needs?

The people of St. George have approved bond issues for new schools because we've been convinced of the need for them. However, we see no reason to spend more money on a mayor and councilmen who are living comfortably on incomes from other sources. When they campaigned for their city positions, they were promised no increases in salary. If they really believe they're worth more than they're getting, they could at least lower their sights to a more realistic level!

Sally Jacobsen, *The Spectrum,* July 14, 1996

67. **Proof That God Does Not Exist**

(Several philosophers have become famous for their proofs that God exists. All those proofs have been theoretical. Here is a practical proof supplied by Dr. E that God does not exist. It can be repeated—try it yourself!)

I go into the Sahara Hotel and Casino in Las Vegas. I go up to the Megabucks slot machine at which you can win at least five million dollars on a $3 bet if you hit the jackpot. I put in three one-dollar coins. I pull the handle. I win nothing, or just a little, and when I continue I lose that, too. Therefore, God does not exist.

68. **Pascal's Wager**

(Pascal was a 17th Century mathematician and philosopher who had a religious conversion late in his life. His argument was roughly as follows.)

We have the choice to believe in God or not to believe in God. If God does not exist, you lose nothing by believing in him. But if He exists, and you believe in him, you have the possibility of eternal life, joyous in the presence of God. If you don't believe in him, you are definitely precluded from having everlasting life. Therefore, a prudent gambler will bet on God existing. That is, it is better to believe that God exists, since you lose nothing by doing so, but could gain everlasting life.

69. **Betting on the Lottery**

The lottery pays millions of dollars. That's more than you can earn with a college degree. The money you spend on tuition could buy lots of tickets. The more tickets you buy, the better your odds of winning. So invest in lottery tickets, not in a dead-end diploma.

70. **On the plans being made to move some of the nearly extinct condors that have been bred in captivity to a wild area in the south of Utah.**

Letter to the editor:

I do not know why we do not leave things alone. Probably environmentalists must have something to show for their reason to exist; often as stupid as wilderness laws by government to make us think they care, for what? Easy money? Now they intend to move condors to Utah. Our over-taxed taxpayers should be getting weary of financing so much for the amusement of idiots.

As long as I can remember, the wolves, elk and now the condor and other nonhuman species have been pawns on the environmental checkerboard for no reason except the whim of a loon to change the order of the universe. I would think all creatures have the instinct to move if they so desired without any help. I am sure the place of their choice would be better for them if not made by us. Let us grow up and leave the elk, wolves and condors alone and mind our own business

Kenneth S. Frandsen, *The Spectrum,* March, 1996

71. **America's Next Hostage Crisis?**

According to the latest figures, America is now importing almost 50 percent of all the oil we use. If our oil imports continue to rise, another energy crisis could be triggered, one that could hold America's economy hostage again.

But the more we use nuclear energy, instead of imported oil, to generate electricity, the less we have to depend on foreign nations.

Our 112 nuclear electric plants already have cut foreign oil dependence by 4 billion barrels since the oil embargo of 1973, saving us more than $115 billion in foreign oil payments. But 112 nuclear plants will not be enough to meet our growing electricity demand. More plants are needed.

We can help keep America from being held hostage and maintain our energy independence by relying more on our own resources, like nuclear energy.

For a free booklet on nuclear energy, write to the U.S. Council for Energy Awareness, P.O. Box 66103, Dept. RF07, Washington, D.C. 20035.

Nuclear energy means more energy independence.   ©1989 USCEA

A Basketball Star ... (Exercises 72–75)

(During the 1995-1996 professional basketball season, a player for the Denver Nuggets, Mahmoud Abdul-Rauf, chose not to stand during the playing of the national anthem. No one noticed for a long time during the season, but when it was brought to the attention of the management, Abdul-Rauf was given the choice of standing for the anthem or being suspended. He chose to be suspended from playing. He explained that he would not stand for religious reasons. Later in the season he was convinced by Muslim religious authorities that it would not contravene his religious principles to stand during the anthem, and he chose to do that while silently praying. His suspension was lifted.)

72. To the editor:

The former Chris Jackson, now known as Mahmoud Abdul-Rauf, refuses to stand for the national anthem. He claims "The Star-Spangled Banner" is a symbol of oppression and tyranny. He insists on discrediting our country even though he is being paid more than $2.5 million a year ($31,707 per game) to play professional basketball.

This young man should really show his disdain for our tyrannical country by giving up his millionaire status and moving to the Middle East where he can seek empathy for his beliefs and he won't have to worry about hearing our beloved national anthem!

Robert E. Haynes, *Las Vegas Review-Journal,* March 24, 1996

73. To the editor:

If Denver Nuggets player Mahmoud Abdul-Rauf feels he is oppressed in the United States he should go play for one of the famous Muslim basketball teams such as the Iranian Jackals, the Bangladesh Bengals or the Bosnian Rockets, etc.

Maybe we should do what they would do if he made comments there, such as he is allowed to do in our "oppressed" country–cut his tongue out.

William J. Musso, *Las Vegas Review-Journal,* March 24, 1996

74. To the editor:

Mahmoud Abdul-Rauf will now stand for the national anthem. Can anyone out there tell me they believe something has happened in this country that has caused a change of heart in this young man where he now wishes to show respect for the flag and national anthem? It is my belief that Mr. Abdul-Rauf has no more respect today than the day he decided to take his stance.

While Mr. Abdul-Rauf has become the focus of this issue, I believe the NBA and its rule should be. Flag-burners show no less respect for the flag than the NBA rules. While a flag-burner expresses contempt for the freedom that allows his expression, the NBA rule shows the same contempt for freedom by forcing an expression of respect.

This conjures up images of the dark side of nationalism–the dark side being forced nationalism. In the 20th century this country has fought two world wars against a form of forced nationalism.

While the government cannot and should not interfere here in any way with the NBA and its rules, we as private citizens should make our voices heard. The next time I see players and coaches standing for the national anthem, the image of the NBA will be more of a Nazi Germany than of a free society.

Terry E. Peele, *Las Vegas Review-Journal,* March 24, 1996

75. **Local radio plays national anthem at mosque**

Islamic leaders were angered Wednesday after a local radio personality played the national anthem on a trumpet at a mosque during a live broadcast to mock a Denver Nuggets basketball player who is a convert to Islam.

Islamic worshippers were praying at the mosque when the radio personality, who donned a turban, wore an Abdul-Rauf T-shirt and carried a trumpet, entered the Colorado Muslim Society Islamic Center on Tuesday with two other employees.

"One of the intruders held a microphone as they were broadcasting live on a local radio station," the report from the sheriff's office said.

The intruders tried to place earphones on two worshippers at the mosque and force them to be part of a live interview. *Reuters Ltd.,* March, 1996

(What implicit argument were the DJs making?)

76. **Sailors imprisoned for rape**

(Concerning the rape of a school girl by three U.S. sailors in Okinawa)
Letter to the editor:

Judging by your opinionated editorial about the Navy, it appears your paper is entirely governed by women for you do not have the slightest conception of what men are all about. But several points need emphasizing:

1. All human beings are animals, and sex is an integral part of their well-being.

2. When a man meets a woman, his thoughts go quickly past the beauty of her eyes and the color of her hair, certainly the capabilities of her brain. That comes later! In 1995, many women have the same thoughts about men.

3. Soldiers, especially sailors who have been at sea for a long time, have a libido that's healthy and must be sustained in order to function normally. Ask any veteran to confirm what precedes.

4. A prostitute has never been called a decent woman in any language. She is still a whore who gets paid for a job well-done. Thank you! It's her choosing, not that of the men at large.

Now, rape is another thing. It is strictly about sex but it is perpetrated by devious minds who could not care about whom they violate, man or woman. Subjugation of the female . . . my foot! What counts is sexual satisfaction, nothing else.

Admiral Macke was honest when he declared it was stupid of his sailors to have raped the Japanese girl when they could have afforded a girl for the price of the rented car. His remark was not unbelievable; it was just. It had nothing to do with the act itself. It was a statement of fact.

This society encourages hypocrisy. The admiral was right and brave enough to declare his assumption in public. He should have been commended for his fortitude in viewing the world the way it really is, not what it portrays.

Rene Vergught, *The Spectrum,* December 21, 1995

77. **Timber wars: Even rotting logs have rights, don't they?**

The stars came out in Carlotta, Calif., as protesters yipped and screamed about plans to salvage rotting timber from beneath a privately owned grove of ancient redwood trees.

Millionaire celebrities, including singers Bonnie Raitt and Don Henley, joined perhaps 1,000 others to raise a major ruckus outside the gates of Pacific Lumber Co.'s Carlotta mill, north of San Francisco. A bunch of them got arrested, some chained themselves to gates, one guy stuck his hand in a bucket of cement, and many engaged in a species of ululating they call "wailing women."

At issue is Pacific Lumber's plan to remove dead logs and diseased trees from the 3,000 acres that it owns in the Headwaters Forest. The company has no designs on the old-growth redwoods on its property. It wants only to clean out the dead and dying stuff and mill the lumber. All the relevant authorities have approved the salvage operation.

But the greens are having none of it. Dragging out the dead stuff might endanger living trees, they claim, and it might disrupt the lifestyles of some woodland creatures.

The protesters have managed to delay Pacific's salvage operation.

Question: If dead wood cannot be harvested on private land because doing so would disrupt the habitat of animals that are not even endangered—can dead trees be salvaged anywhere? Can live trees on private land be cut anywhere? Every tree is a habitat for some critter or other.

It should be obvious by now that hard-core environmentalists want no forests anywhere touched for any commercial reason—ever. If, as a consequence, the timber industry dies completely, lumber becomes rare and you end up paying $3 million for a $100,000 house, $40 a copy for a newspaper or $25,000 for a kitchen cabinet—tough.

If these millionaire celebrities care so deeply about rotting logs on Pacific Lumber's land, why don't they buy it?   Editorial, *Las Vegas Review-Journal,* September, 1996

78. **High School Wrestling**

Pine View High School officials chose the only reasonable position when they decided to deny a 17-year-old girl's petition to join the school's all-male wrestling team. Technically, the school was within its legal rights to deny the request, according to the U. S. Office of Civil Rights. While the federal law involved, known as Title IX, requires equality in a school's overall athletic program, it also permits schools to keep girls out of "contact" sports such as football and wrestling.

Wrestling is, without question, a contact sport. Lots and lots of body contact. That's kind of the point of the sport—to wrestle and pin your opponent to the mat. You can't do that unless you do a lot of grabbing, clutching, poking, holding, groping, flipping, and generally, having some really solid, personal, one-on-one contact with someone else's body.

Common sense tells us this is one sport where girls and boys should compete separately.

Pine View High School Principal David Broadhead said the school has a strong girl's athletics program, giving girls the chance to earn a letter in various sports. One sport denied to girls, however, is wrestling.

And with good reason. Until there are enough girls who indicate they want to participate in such a sport—and enough to set up girls-only teams to compete against each other—it only makes sense to keep girls out of this male-dominated field.

It's a shame that this particular student won't have the chance to pursue her dream of lettering in wrestling at Pine View High School.

We sympathize and certainly understand the desire to follow a dream. It's an admirable quality and shouldn't be lightly dismissed.

But, the greater question in this debate isn't whether a girl should be allowed on a boy's wrestling team, but whether the girl's athletic programs here are treated equally and given the same kind of support within the school system.

Editorial, *The Spectrum,* July 13, 1997

79. **Prairie Dogs**

Just about every time the word "prairie dog" is mentioned anymore in Iron County, there is heated debate.

Biology professor Jim Bowns discussed prairie dogs during a meeting sponsored by the Color Country Chapter of People for the West in Cedar City Thursday night. Bowns is a professor for both Southern Utah University and Utah State University.

Prairie dogs are a threatened species in Southern Utah. There has been quite a bit of argument in Iron County over how to preserve the little critters without creating chaos.

Iron County is working on a Habitat Conservation Plan (HCP) otherwise known as the Prairie Dog Plan. The HCP will serve as a blanket application for people to safely remove prairie dogs from their land without all the red tape.

Bowns dissected the HCP page by page, voicing his concerns and explaining jargon to the audience. Several discussions ensued during the process.

Bowns said he is especially concerned with prairie dog habitat.

"Finding ideal habitat for prairie dogs is not simple," he said.

The prairie dogs usually have about a 6 percent survival rate, a 94 percent loss, he continued, reading from the HCP.

Lin Drake appeared unhappy at this statement. He is a developer and an officer for the Color Country Chapter of People for the West.

If he lost 94 percent of his business, Drake explained that the bank sure wouldn't be accommodating.

"Yet they're expecting Iron County to put millions of dollars into a project that is a losing cause," he said. . . .

Throughout the discussion, the topic of government distrust surfaced and resurfaced.

"Eighteen people came to me this week to talk about the plan," Jack Hill said. Hill is president of the Color Country Chapter of People for the West.

"They have a lack of faith in the federal government and they don't have any trust," Hill said. "The whole issue is with the government."

Drake agreed, saying the HCP appears to weaken his rights to his land. He would prefer the government back off and worry about more important things, he said.

"We've got fathers beating babies and drugs on the streets and we're spending money on this," Drake said. "Tell them to get the hell out of Iron County." . . .

Drake was disappointed at the turnout of the meeting. Only a dozen people attended, though the meeting was advertised adequately.

"They'll wake up when we don't have a community left," he said.
(Note: June 26, 1997 Lin Drake was fined $15,000 by the U.S. Fish and Wildlife Service for putting a subdivision on a prairie dog habitat.)

The Spectrum, April 18, 1997

80. **Inmate Phone Center**

The Utah Travel Council's recent announcement that it plans to hire inmates housed at the Utah State Prison to field travel questions and take orders for brochures sounds like an idea destined to fail.

Spencer Kinard, assistant director for the travel council, had the audacity to make a tasteless joke about the proposal, saying, "You're going to have your favorite serial killer giving you information about where to go."

If that comment isn't enough to put a bad taste in your mouth, consider the fact that since the first of the year, inmates have been typing into computers the names and addresses of recorded requests for brochures and travel guides.

Raise your hand if you want your name and address given to a convict. It's unanimous. There are no takers.

Another poorly thought-out comment came from the travel center director, Dean Reeder, who said using inmates for a labor pool was a good idea because of their low turnover and their untapped work skill.

That's not a good enough reason to let inmates have access to personal information. It's hard to imagine a dumber idea.

Both Kinard and Reeder are employees of the State Department of Community and Economic Development. That means their salaries are paid with public money and that they are using public funds to conduct this mindless experiment.

Taxpayers should revolt over this one.

Five states have apparently experimented with such an idea and have reported mixed results. Oklahoma ended a similar program when prisoners became adept at giving out the 1-800 information lines to family and friends.

Kinard, on the other hand, thinks the idea constitutes a grand experiment and should ferret out some smart criminals who are fairly bright and who were involved in white collar crime. As if those types of crimes don't involve victims, too.

So far, the Travel Council has kept a tight lid on its plans and has not sought the feedback of regional partners whose attractions would be touted by the inmate phone centers.

Big mistake.

The plans call for a slow start and possible expansion. All inmates who are not in lock down status or considered security risks would be eligible to apply for the job. The Travel Council says the idea is a creative solution to a simple problem of not enough money and too much work. It handles nearly 100,000 information requests a year.

It's doubtful those callers will approve of the Travel Council's grand experiment to solve its money woes. Reed and Kinard say they're bracing themselves for raised eyebrows as details of the plan take shape next month.

Anyone with a brain the size of an ant should do more than raise an eyebrow at this half-baked idea. The Utah Travel Council should confine this idea to solitary and leave it locked up there . . . forever.

Editorial, The Spectrum, June 3, 1997

81. Police chief's dumping a dumb deed by North Las Vegas

North Las Vegas cannot afford to lose any IQ points—especially in the area of law enforcement—and that's exactly what happened with the forced retirement of city Police Chief Alan Nelson. A 25-year veteran, Nelson was arrested Friday on a drunken driving charge. Rather than battle it out in the courts and attempt to play politics with the North Las Vegas City Council, Mayor James Seastrand and City Manager Linda Hinson, Nelson cleared off his desk and turned in his badge.

That's a shame.

If I may be so presumptuous, the people of North Las Vegas—hard-working people who live in one of the nation's high-crime areas—need police officers of Nelson's experience and level. I'm not condoning driving while legally impaired—although it would be refreshing to read the department's official lab findings before seeing the Northtown political machine bury the chief's career without even playing "Taps."

It makes painfully little sense to force him out of office in the name of political correctness and image enhancement. Holding a top police officer to a higher standard is fine, but this presses the point to the extreme.

If the man has a drinking problem, he should be treated with compassion—not a pink slip. After all, it's not as if he is the first cop to drive drunk, if he did.

Fact is, if he were anyone but the chief and were arrested and later convicted, of driving while intoxicated, Nelson probably would have received a 40-hour suspension and, like almost everyone else similarly situated, would have been ordered by the court to attend alcohol-awareness classes and seek rehabilitation.

Imagine the image Nelson might have enhanced had he been asked to cut a few public-service announcements for anti-DUI groups?

That's not possible now.

Nelson has plenty of critics these days, but he also has his share of friends. North Las Vegas Police Lt. Bob King is one of them. With nearly 26 years on the department, King is the Narcotics Division commander. He knows sticking up for his ousted comrade is unlikely to win him any points with the city's political hierarchy.

"He's not a high-profiler. He's one of those guys who has been in the trenches, kind of a worker bee," King says. "It just breaks my heart, the whole thing. He was really beginning to move the department forward. He was doing all these good things. And he has one transgression, if you will, four blocks from his house."

Be honest. If you were the top cop in one of the nation's roughest communities, wouldn't you be tempted to drink?

Arsenic.

That doesn't mitigate the seriousness of the offense, but neither should the offense wipe out a quarter century of hard work.

As chief, Nelson was implementing the progressive Safe Streets 2000 community policing program and, King says, was a fair-minded administrator who had a mature grasp of the budget realities the small department faced. He also understood the convoluted federal government grant-writing process, an essential component in the budget mechanism in many departments. North Las Vegas has fewer than 200 cops on the street.

"Those talents are gone," King says. "When he gave his word, you knew he was there for you. You knew exactly where he stood day to day. He has my respect, appreciation and admiration."

In an open letter, King adds, "I see a man whose entire 25-year professional career of personal contributions and accomplishments as both an outstanding policeman and administrator are totally overshadowed and will be measured by a single regrettable incident. . . . He neither asked for nor received any preferential treatment. He practiced and demonstrated this ethic his entire career. With eloquence and dignity he has left the job he dearly loves."

For all his human frailties, Chief Nelson was a hard-working cop who was dumped in the name of political correctness. In North Las Vegas, yet.

And that's just plain dumb.

John L. Smith, March 20, 1997, Las Vegas Review-Journal

82. **Dumb deed**

In his March 20 column ("Police chief dumping a dumb deed by North Las Vegas"), John L. Smith used sarcastic remarks to assess the situation pertaining to North Las Vegas and its former chief of police, Alan Nelson.

But the only "dumb deed" in North Las Vegas was created by its former police chief when he chose to drink and drive. And let's not forget the "dumb deed" was further enhanced by the fact he was driving a city vehicle. It is also dumb for people to minimize the seriousness of drinking and driving by singing the praises of a potential killer. How potential? If a driver's blood-alcohol level is .10 the risk of a fatal crash is increased by 300 percent. Mr. Nelson's chemical test revealed his BAC level to be at .12.

And consider this: The profile of a drunken driver includes the fact that DUI offenders drive drunk an average of 80 times per year.

The "dumb" continues—"He wasn't drunk," "It's only a misdemeanor," "A single regrettable incident," "He has one transgression" . . . these are the reasons I have heard and read in defense of Mr. Nelson. This mentality is nearly as frightening as the crime of DUI. "A single regrettable incident" and "one transgression" on the part of drinking drivers was all it took in 1996 to cause the death and injury of more than 1,600 people in Clark County.

Mr. Smith suggested certain IQ points were lost by North Las Vegas and he also alluded to that city's need for police officers of Mr. Nelson's experience. Based on the numerous calls I received from the citizens of North Las Vegas, I believe they want officers at that experience level to also possess an IQ that would not allow jeopardizing a 25-year career nor permit conduct that would endanger the citizens.

Mr. Smith agreed that holding "top police officers" to a higher standard is fine—but he said "political correctness" has gone too far in this instance. Political correctness? Has our society strayed so far from the realm of social, moral and ethical responsibilities that when these standards are utilized, they are scoffed at as "political correctness"?

As far as Mr. Nelson's "forced retirement" is concerned, I can only say that if I had dedicated a quarter of a century of my life to a career and was wrongly accused of a crime that would have a negative effect on that career, I would fight like hell to vindicate myself. Again, that is only if I were wrongly accused.

I question whether Mr. Smith's commentary would have been as generous and compassionate if he and his beautiful child whom he wrote so eloquently about not so long ago had been in the path of Mr. Nelson the night he was arrested (assuming they lived to write about it). Never forget there is only one thing that separates a felony from a misdemeanor—it's called luck.

Mr. Smith stated that if Mr. Nelson has a drinking problem he should be treated with compassion. If he has a "drinking problem," why wasn't it recognized by his friends and co-workers? How could he be treated if the stale, antiquated "drinking problem" excuse is deemed not to be applicable?

If you want to hear "Taps," Mr. Smith, come to our next DUI Victims Candlelight Vigil. You have attended before—however, it appears you may have forgotten the victims who were there. Let me refresh your memory. They were the people who were sobbing their guts out in memory of their loved ones who had been killed by people like Alan Nelson. Your seat is reserved.

Sandy Heverly, president of Stop DUI, a Nevada non-profit organization.

Las Vegas Review-Journal, April 9, 1997

Writing Lesson 13

For each of the following write the best argument you can that has as conclusion the claim below the cartoon. List only the premises and conclusion. If you believe the best argument is only weak, explain why. Do not make up a story about the cartoon. Use what you see in the cartoon and your common knowledge.

1.

Manuel is in an Olympic race for the handicapped.

2.

Flo is lying.

3.

Professor Zzzyzzx hit the wasps' nest.

4.

An adult who is not a fireman opened the fire hydrant.

12 Reasoning by Analogy

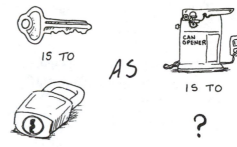

IS TO

AS

IS TO

?

Key Words   reasoning by analogy

Exercises for Chapter 12

1. Some indicator words that suggest an analogy is being used are "like," "just as," "for the same reason." List three more.

2. What do you need to make a comparison into reasoning by analogy?

3. Are analogies typically complete arguments? Explain.

4. What should you do first in evaluating an analogy? Second?

Tom's caught on to the idea of how to evaluate analogies pretty well. Here are some of the exercises he did.

> **You should treat dogs humanely. How would you feel if you were caged up all day and experimented on? Or if you were chained to a stake all day? Or someone beat you every time you did something wrong?**

Argument? (yes or no) Yes.

Conclusion: You should treat dogs humanely.

Comparison: I'm not certain, cause they stated most of it as questions. But it seems they're comparing being a dog and being treated badly with you being treated badly, like getting caged up all day, or chained to a stake all day, or someone beating you every time you did something wrong.

Wrong   Wrong

Premises: Most of this is unstated. We're just supposed to put down what's actually said here, which I guess would be:

You shouldn't cage up a person all day.

You shouldn't chain a person to a stake all day.

You shouldn't beat someone every time she does something wrong.

People are like dogs.

So you shouldn't do any of that to dogs.

Similarities: I know we're supposed to pick out ones that'll give us a general principle. I've got to figure out how dogs and humans are similar. Well, dogs and humans are both mammals. Perhaps that'll do: "You shouldn't mistreat any mammal."

Additional premises needed to make it valid or strong (if none, say so): Dogs and humans are both mammals. You shouldn't mistreat any mammal.

Classify (with the additional premises): <u>valid</u>   very strong ————— weak

Good argument? I don't know. I guess the added premises are O.K. So probably it's pretty good.

Good work. You've got the basis of the analogy right. You understand the method. You've picked out a general principle—but is it true? After all, cats are mammals—does that mean we should treat them humanely?

There's one clue you overlooked. They said, "How would you feel . . ." I can imagine how it would feel to be a dog and be mistreated, just as I can imagine how it would feel to be

you and be mistreated (sort of, not exactly of course). How about:

    We can imagine what it would be like to be a dog.

    We should treat humanely any creature that we can imagine what it would feel like to be mistreated.

That's more plausible, because it rules out cats. And it might include fish, which some people think should be treated humanely.

    But really, you did O.K. We're unsure how to repair the original argument because it's too sketchy.

It is easier for a camel to go through the eye of a needle than for a rich man to enter into the kingdom of God.

Argument? (yes or no) This is from the Bible, right? I think it's supposed to make us think that being rich is bad. But I'm not sure. I can't figure out a conclusion, so I better say it's not an argument.

Conclusion (if unstated, add it):

Comparison:

Premises: *Good work!*

Similarities:

Additional premises (make the comparison explicit, add a general principle):

Classify (with the additional premises): valid   very strong ——————— weak

Good argument? (look for differences or ways the general principle could be false)

Critical thinking is like learning to drive a car. It requires practice—you can't just learn it as theory. That's why I give you so many messy arguments to analyze.

Argument? (yes or no) Yes, but just barely.

Conclusion (if unstated, add it): You should have lots of messy arguments to analyze in doing critical thinking.

Comparison: Critical thinking isn't at all like driving a car. Driving a car is a kind of physical skill, like playing basketball. Critical thinking is something you strain your brain over. Sure you need practice on hard stuff till it gets routine. But I don't see how messy arguments are anything like driving a car.

Premises:

Similarities:

Additional premises (make the comparison explicit, add a general principle):

Classify (with the additional premises): valid   very strong ——————— weak

Good argument? (look for differences or ways the general principle could be false)

    I think it's pretty bad. I can't figure out what general principle you'd want.

    Good—you jumped to the punch line. There may be something in this comparison, but it's not clear yet, and you're justified in stopping here.

Here are some comparisons for you to evaluate. Note that there may be more than one argument in an example.

5.   You wouldn't buy a kitten at a pet store to give to your dog. Why, then, do you consider it acceptable to buy white rats for your boa constrictor?

Argument? (yes or no)

Conclusion (if unstated, add it):

Comparison:

Premises:

Similarities:

Additional premises (make the comparison explicit, add a general principle):

Classify (with the additional premises):   valid   very strong ——————— weak

Good argument? (look for differences or ways the general principle could be false)

6.   All the world's a stage and the men and women merely players.

Argument? (yes or no)

Conclusion (if unstated, add it):

Comparison:

Premises:

Similarities:

Additional premises (make the comparison explicit, add a general principle):

Classify (with the additional premises):   valid   very strong ——————— weak

Good argument? (look for differences or ways the general principle could be false)

7. Dick: Zoe, let's get married.
   Zoe: I've told you before, Dick, I won't get married until we sleep together.
   Dick: But that would be wrong. I won't sleep with you before we get married.
   Zoe: Would you buy a car without a test drive?
   Dick: Why buy the cow when the milk's free?

   Argument? (yes or no)
   Conclusion (if unstated, add it):

   Comparison:

   Premises:

   Similarities:

   Additional premises (make the comparison explicit, add a general principle):

   Classify (with the additional premises):   valid   very strong ——————— weak

   Good argument? (look for differences or ways the general principle could be false)

8. (In Japan in 1996 there was a debate whether the U.S. military bases should be allowed
   to remain on the island of Okinawa. Just a few years previously, the U.S. closed its base
   in the Philippines after the Philippine government requested it to do so.)

   U.S. and Japanese leaders have stressed the necessity of keeping U.S. troops on
   the island to assure security in the region.
   　　　But [Governor of Okinawa Masahide] Ota disagrees. "When the U.S. had bases
   in the Philippines, they used to emphasize that they were [militarily] indispensable," he
   said. "But they abandoned them, and nothing happened."

   Associated Press, March 6, 1996

   Argument? (yes or no)

Conclusion (if unstated, add it):

Comparison:

Premises:

Similarities:

Additional premises (make the comparison explicit, add a general principle):

Classify (with the additional premises):   valid   very strong ——————— weak
Good argument? (look for differences or ways the general principle could be false)

9. If killing is wrong, why do you punish murderers by killing them?
    Argument? (yes or no)
    Conclusion (if unstated, add it):

Comparison:

Premises:

Similarities:

Additional premises (make the comparison explicit, add a general principle):

Classify (with the additional premises):   valid   very strong ——————— weak
Good argument? (look for differences or ways the general principle could be false)

10. Maria: The college is collecting parking fees from us as part of our student fees, but we're not getting anything for it. We have to park a long way from our classes, so far we might as well park in the free lot. And the parking garage they promised us won't be built while we're here. We're not getting our money's worth. It would be wrong if you went to a mall and paid for a CD and then they didn't give it to you, or if you paid for a carwash and they left the car dirty. The college should discontinue the fee and refund what we've already paid.

Argument? (yes or no)
Conclusion (if unstated, add it):

Comparison:

Premises:

Similarities:

Additional premises (make the comparison explicit, add a general principle):

Classify (with the additional premises):   valid   very strong ——————— weak
Good argument? (look for differences or ways the general principle could be false)

11. All the conspicuous features on the surface of the moon are the result of impacts. These features include not only the craters, which plainly advertise their origins, but also the great maria, or "seas," which are craters that filled with lava following the impact of very massive objects. Most of the impacts took place during a relatively brief period about four billion years ago, when debris left over from the formation of the solar system was swept up by the planets and their satellites. The earth probably received as heavy a pelting as the moon did, and it therefore must have been densely cratered.

"Science and the Citizen," *Scientific American,* June, 1976

Argument? (yes or no)
Conclusion (if unstated, add it):

Comparison:

Premises:

Similarities:

Additional premises (make the comparison explicit, add a general principle):

Classify (with the additional premises):   valid   very strong ——————— weak

Good argument? (look for differences or ways the general principle could be false)

12. A ban on handguns won't deter crime. After all, making drugs illegal doesn't work.
Argument? (yes or no)
Conclusion (if unstated, add it):

Comparison:

Premises:

Similarities:

Additional premises (make the comparison explicit, add a general principle):

Classify (with the additional premises):   valid   very strong ——————— weak
Good argument? (look for differences or ways the general principle could be false)

13. I know I can't really feel a pain you have. But because we're so much alike in so many ways, I'm sure that you feel physical pain in much the same way I do.
Argument? (yes or no)
Conclusion (if unstated, add it):

Comparison:

Premises:

Similarities:

Additional premises (make the comparison explicit, add a general principle):

Classify (with the additional premises):   valid   very strong —————————— weak

Good argument? (look for differences or ways the general principle could be false)

14. If we regulate the use of Ebonics, then will we have to regulate Western slang in the school system.

    Argument? (yes or no)

    Conclusion (if unstated, add it):

    Comparison:

    Premises:

    Similarities:

    Additional premises (make the comparison explicit, add a general principle):

    Classify (with the additional premises):   valid   very strong —————————— weak

    Good argument? (look for differences or ways the general principle could be false)

15. Dick: How hard can it be to raise kids? After all, I've trained two dogs.

    Argument? (yes or no)

    Conclusion (if unstated, add it):

    Comparison:

    Premises:

    Similarities:

Additional premises (make the comparison explicit, add a general principle):

Classify (with the additional premises):   valid   very strong ——————— weak

Good argument? (look for differences or ways the general principle could be false)

16. God must exist. The way everything works together in nature, the adaptation of means to ends, the beauty, resembles but far exceeds what men do. Everything works together as a fine piece of machinery. So there must be some maker with intelligence behind all of nature. That is, God exists and is similar to human mind and intelligence.

Argument? (yes or no)

Conclusion (if unstated, add it):

Comparison:

Premises:

Similarities:

Additional premises (make the comparison explicit, add a general principle):

Classify (with the additional premises):   valid   very strong ——————— weak

Good argument? (look for differences or ways the general principle could be false)

17. **Bride busted for drinking at her OWN wedding**
Wheatland, Wyo. – A new bride faces up to $750 in fines and six months in jail–for having a drink at her own wedding reception!

Jennifer Windemeir, who was 20 years and 7 months old at the time–under the state's legal drinking age of 21– was charged with being a minor in possession of alcohol after an off-duty cop spotted her taking a sip.

"This is absurd," blasts the bride's attorney Eric Alden. "Why anyone would take what's supposed to be the happiest day of someone's life and try to turn it into a crime is beyond me."

The legal drama unfolded about 9:30 p.m. on February 3, a couple of weeks after Jennifer and new husband David were married in a civil ceremony. "It was a two-phase reception," says Alden.

"The first phase was at a church. Later a party of about 20 of the younger guests headed to the Mine Restaurant and Lounge.

"Guests proposed toasts to the bride and groom, and Jennifer took a sip from what I understand was a glass of white wine."

Sheriff's Deputy John Matthews, who was at the lounge with his wife, recognized Jennifer and thought she was underage, said Alden. "The next day he ran a driver's license check and interviewed the barmaid about what she'd served the table."

Three weeks later Jennifer was notified she was being charged. "She was really upset and came to me in tears," says Alden. "I agreed to represent her for free as a wedding gift." The lawyer argues that politics were behind the charges against Jennifer, who's the daughter of the local sheriff. "Deputy Matthews' uncle had run against Jennifer's dad and lost. I assume he was PO'd and this was a way to embarrass the sheriff."

The officer's wife Rhonda gives a different version of events.

"The reception was over and Jennifer and her husband were just in the bar hanging out and drinking tequila," she insists.

"Everyone else in town has to be 21 to drink. Just because she's the sheriff's daughter doesn't make her above the law."

But Alden vows to battle the charges, which go to trial mid-June. "What's next? Are cops going to kick down church doors and drag kids away from the communion rail for drinking wine?"

Weekly World News, June 11, 1996

Argument? (yes or no)

Conclusion (if unstated, add it):

Comparison:

Premises:

Similarities:

Additional premises (make the comparison explicit, add a general principle):

Classify (with the additional premises):   valid   very strong ——————— weak

Good argument? (look for differences or ways the general principle could be false)

18. The following editorial is an argument. Answer the questions at the end.

Voters in Arizona and California approved ballot measures Nov. 5 allowing prescription of marijuana and other controlled substances for certain patients.

The most prevalent use is to ease the suffering of terminal patients or to counteract the side effects of chemotherapy . . .

The legal effect of the measures' passage is still up in the air, since the uses remain outlawed under federal statute. But retired General Barry McCaffrey, the White House's drug policy director, is quite certain about what the practical effect will be:

"Increased drug abuse in every category will be the inevitable result of the referenda," he said in a speech last week. "There could not be a worse message to young people than the provisions of these referenda . . . They are being told that marijuana and other drugs are good, they are medicine."

Apply this logic to the general's primary area of expertise:

Does the necessity of maintaining a standing army and engaging in war to protect national interests send a message to teens to arm themselves and form street gangs?

. . . There is a line between use and abuse of a necessary evil like lethal force or a powerful narcotic.

Social, economic and political circumstances justify the use of lethal force in war; medical circumstances justify the use of drugs.

But to think that teens or other forms of life lower on the food chain than generals are unable to differentiate between use and abuse may lead directly to the kind of logic under which students are expelled for possession of over-the-counter analgesics like Midol.

Albuquerque Journal, November 19, 1996

a. What is its conclusion?

b. What analogy does the editorial make?

c. How does it use the methods for evaluating analogies?

d. Are there any slanters or bad argument types?

e. Is the argument good?

19. a. Suppose that tomorrow good, highly reliable research is announced showing that oils derived from eyelids removed without anesthetic from healthy cats when applied to human skin reduced wrinkles significantly. Would it be justifiable to do further research and manufacture this oil? Explain.

  b. Same as (a) except that the oil is drunk with orange juice and significantly reduced the chance of lung cancer for smokers. Explain.

  c. Same as (a) except the oil is mixed with potatoes and eaten and significantly reduced the chance of heart disease and lengthened the lives of women. Explain.

  d. Same as (a) except that when drunk the oil killed off all viruses harmful to humans. Explain.

20. Do Exercise 19 reading "dogs" for "cats."

Writing Lesson 14

You understand what reasoning by analogy is now. So write an argument *using an analogy* either for or against the following:

"Just as alcohol and tobacco are legal, we should legalize the use of marijuana."

Check whether your instructor has chosen a *DIFFERENT TOPIC* for this assignment.

There are roughly three ways you can argue:

- Marijuana is no worse than alcohol or tobacco, so we should legalize it. (Arguing from similarities.)

- Marijuana is worse than alcohol and tobacco, so we should not legalize it. (Arguing from differences.)

- Marijuana is no worse than alcohol or tobacco, but it is a mistake to have those legal, and we should not make the situation worse by legalizing marijuana. (Arguing from similarities.)

Write the argument as just a *one page* essay. It should be clear and well structured, since you will have written out the claims and diagrammed it first for yourself. You shouldn't have to do major research for this, but at least be sure your premises are plausible.

13   Numbers?

Key Words

apples and oranges   average
two times zero is still zero   mean
phony precision   median
                              mode

Exercises for Chapter 13

1. Find an advertisement that uses a claim with percentages that is misleading or vague or ambiguous.

2. Find an advertisement that uses a claim with numbers other than percentages that is misleading or vague or ambiguous.

3. Compare a sundial on a sunny day and a digital watch that is set wrong.
    a. Which is most accurate at telling the time?

    b. Which is most precise?

4. Find the average, mean, median, and mode of the scores of Dr. E's students who took his critical thinking final exam: 92, 54, 60, 86, 62, 76, 88, 88, 62, 68, 81.
    Average:

    Mean:

    Median:

    Mode:

For Exercises 5–20 point out any use of numbers or percentages that is vague or misleading.

5. Try new Smooth-Glow skin creme, containing a mixture of special oils derived from fava beans. It will reduce your skin's aging by 50%.

6. [Advertisement] Called home lately? 1-800-Collect® Save up to 44%. Savings based on a 3 min. AT&T operator-dialed interstate call.

7. [Advertisement] Era® costs up to 1/3 less than those pricey brands and helps remove your toughest stains.

8. [Advertisement for *3 Musketeers*® candy bars]
    The sweetest part is finding out how little fat it has.
    (45% less fat than the average of the 25 leading chocolate brands, to be exact.)*
        *Not a low-fat food. 8 fat grams per serving for single bar vs. 15 gram average for leading chocolate brands.

9. [Advertisement] Studies have shown that three cups of Cheerios a day with a low fat diet can help lower cholesterol.

10. [Advertisement on box of laundry detergent] 25% more free!

11. The Nevada Dance Festival had a great year in 1993. Attendance was up 22%.

12. The rate of inflation went down 2%.

13. [Concerning the way the U.S. Census Bureau operates] In 1990, 65% of the question-naires that were mailed were filled out and returned. Census counters went back to every household that didn't mail back a form. Even then, the bureau was able to count only 98.4% of the U.S. population.   *USA TODAY,* April 15, 1998

14. [Television ad] More and more doctors are now recommending Advil®.

15. Hey, I just won $800 at this slot machine!

16. Incredible increase in graduation rates of student athletes at our college! Up by 50%!

17. [Advertisement]
    Official Royal Flush Results!   Fiesta 2,115
                                    Texas 1,735

    It's not even close
    Fiesta backs up its claim:

    "We Pay More Royal Flushes per Machine Than Any Other Casino Hotel in the World!"

    For the month of September, Texas claimed that it paid out a total of 1,735 Royals, with approximately 2,000 machines, but for that same period, Fiesta Casino paid out 2,115 Royal Flushes, with just 1,200 machines. Here's proof, once again, that Fiesta's Slots and Video Poker Machines are the loosest on Earth!

18. **Artery narrowing can be reversed**

A new study has shown what many researchers have thought all along—cardiovascular disease (i.e., narrowing of the arteries) can be moderately reversed.

The well-known secret: lifestyle changes.

In the study, heart patients who had coronary artery (heart) disease—diagnosed through angiograms (X-rays of the arteries)—were: 1) put on a vegetarian diet, 2) told to stop smoking, 3) started on a mild to moderate aerobic exercise program (three hours per week), and 4) told to practice stress management techniques (e.g., meditation) one hour a day.

Five-year findings: In a *control* group of heart patients who had *not* made the above lifestyle changes, 45% had coronary narrowing that became worse; 50% showed no change; and 5% showed improvement.

By comparison, 99% of the group who made significant lifestyle changes (see above) had healthier arteries (i.e., improved blood flow) or their condition remained stable.

From the heart. Washoe Health System, Fall, 1996

19.

20. **S. Korea declares war on leftovers**

Because of the feeling of bounty and plenty that it gives, Koreans routinely cook more at home than they can eat and restaurants serve more than any customer could reasonably consume.

"Koreans are used to thinking 'the more the better,'" said Koh, the restaurant manager.

It's a philosophy the government is battling to change. In the latest round, the government announced Dec. 6 that it will make a major push in 1997 to cut food waste by half.

Many Koreans say they are careful at home to eat leftovers the next day. But restaurant waste, which the government says accounts for 42 percent of food garbage, is a tougher problem.

The government says the country's 45 million people throw away nearly 48,000 metric tons of garbage a day.

Pauline Jelinek, Associated Press, November 23, 1996

21. Dick: I read that on average women think of sex every 18 minutes.
    Zoe: Really? I guess some woman out there is thinking of sex about once a year.

    What is Zoe implying? Does she understand averages correctly?

Which of the following claims should be trusted to give you a good idea of the population as a whole? For which would you prefer to know the median or mode? Explain.

22. The average wage in the U.S. is $28,912.

23. The average wage in one rural county of Utah was $14,117.

24. The average wage of concert pianists in the U.S. is less than the average wage of university professors.

25. The average number of people in a household in Las Vegas is 2.1.

26. The average number of times a 72-year-old man has sex in a week has been determined, by surveys, to be 1.2 .

27. The average GPA of a graduating senior at this college in 1995 was 2.86, while in 1972 it was 2.41.

28. Dick: Which section of English Lit should I take, Zoe, Professor Zzzyzzx's or Professor Glåsütör's?

    Zoe: It doesn't really matter. You can't understand either, and the department info on the sections said the average mark in both their classes was a C.

29. The average income of a woman in the U.S. was only 82% that of a man.

14   Generalizing from Experience

SPOT!

Key Words

generalization	random sample
population	law of large numbers
sample	gambler's fallacy
inductive evidence	hasty generalization
statistical generalization	anecdotal evidence
representative sample	margin of error
biased sample	confidence level
haphazard sample	variation in a population

Exercises for Section A

Here's some of Tom's work on identifying generalizations.

Maria: Every time I've seen a stranger come to Dick's gate, Spot has barked. So Spot will always bark at strangers at Dick's gate.

Generalization? (yes/no) Yes.

Sample: Every time Maria has seen a stranger come to the gate.

Population: Every time a stranger ever comes to Dick's gate when Spot's there.

   Good.

You shouldn't go out with someone from New York. They're all rude and pushy.

Generalization? (yes/no) Yes.

Sample: All the New Yorkers the person has met.

Population: All New Yorkers.

You're too generous. How do you know if the speaker has ever met a New Yorker? Maybe he's just spouting off a prejudice he acquired from his friends. <u>It's not a generalization if you can't identify the sample.</u>

Should we try the new Mexican restaurant on Sun Street? I heard it was pretty good.

Generalization? (yes/no) Yes.

Sample: People who told him it was good.

Population: It will be good food for him, too.

A generalization is an argument, right. But the sample and the population <u>aren't claims</u>— they're groups. The sample here is the times that other people have eaten there (and reported that it was good). The population is all times anyone has or will eat there. It's a past to future generalization.

Fill in after the italics for the exercises that follow.

1. German shepherds have a really good temperament. I know, because lots of my friends and my sister have one.

   Generalization? (yes/no)

   Sample:

   Population:

2. That blasted paper-boy tossed the paper on the lawn again and the sprinklers got it wet. I'm going to call the newspaper.

   Generalization? (yes/no)

   Sample:

   Population:

3. Suzy: I heard you have a Zitochi CD player.
   Maria: Yeah, and I wish I'd never gotten one. It's always breaking down.
   Suzy: Well, I won't get one then, since they're probably all the same.

   Generalization? (yes/no)

   Sample:

   Population:

4. Maria to Zoe: Don't bother to ask Tom to do the dishes. My brother's a football player and no football player will do the dishes.

   Generalization? (yes/no)

   Sample:

   Population:

5. Suzy: Guys are such nitwits.
   Zoe: What do you mean?
   Suzy: Like, they can't even tell when you're down. Emotionally, they're clods. Besides, they just want a girl for her body.
   Zoe: How do you know?
   Suzy: Duh, it's like a cheerleader like me isn't going to have a lot of dates?

Generalization? (yes/no)

Sample:

Population:

6. Suzy: Are you taking Spot for a walk?
   Zoe: No. I'm getting the leash because I have to take him to the vet, and it will be hard to get him to go. Every time I take him to the vet he seems to know it before we get in the car.

   Generalization? (yes/no)

   Sample:

   Population:

7. You'd better not take the cat in the car with you. She barfed all over your lap last time.

   Generalization? (yes/no)

   Sample:

   Population:

8. Zoe: Do you know a good dry cleaner around here?
   Dick: The one in the plaza north of campus is pretty good. They've always done O.K. with the stuff I take them.

   Generalization? (yes/no)

   Sample:

   Population:

9. Don't go to Mexico in July. It's awfully hot there then.

   Generalization? (yes/no)

   Sample:

   Population:

10. Dogs can be trained to retrieve a newspaper.

    Generalization? (yes/no)

    Sample:

    Population:

11. I want to marry a Japanese guy. They're hard-working and really family oriented.

    Generalization? (yes/no)

    Sample:

    Population:

12. It's incredible how many people in the U.S. watch Baywatch. It got the highest Nielsen ratings of any show on TV.

    Generalization? (yes/no)

    Sample:

    Population:

13. Isabel: I'm so excited. Suzy's arranged a blind-date for me with a football player. I've seen all the games, and the guys on the team are *so* sexy!

    Generalization? (yes/no)

    Sample:

    Population:

14. From our study it appears that the levels of cholesterol in the blood of bald men is lower than that in men with a full head of hair.

    Generalization? (yes/no)

    Sample:

    Population:

15. Write down three examples of generalizations you have heard or made in the last week and one example of a claim that sounds like a generalization and isn't. See if your classmates can pick out the one that isn't. For the generalizations, ask a classmate to identify the sample and the population.

Exercises for Sections B.1 and B.2

1. What is a representative sample?

2. Explain why a good generalization is unlikely to be valid.

3. a. What is the law of large numbers?

    b. How does the law of large numbers justify random sampling as giving unbiased samples?

4. Why does the phone ring more often when you're in the shower?

5. Which of the following seem too biased to be reliable, and why?

    a. To determine the average number of people in your city who engaged in sexual intercourse last week, interview women only.

    b. To determine what kind of cat food is purchased most often, interview only people who have telephones.

    c. To determine what percentage of women think that bald men are sexy, poll students as they leave their classes at your school.

d.   To determine whether to buy grapes at the supermarket, pick a grape from the bunch you're interested in and taste it.

6.   a.   Suppose you want to find out whether people in your city believe that there are enough policemen. Give four characteristics of people that could bias the survey. That is, list four subgroups of the population that you would not want to have represented out of proportion to their actual percentages in the population.

     b.   Now list four characteristics that you feel would not matter for giving bias.

7.   A colleague suggested to me that the best way to get a sample is to select one whose relevant characteristics (e.g., gender, age, ethnicity, income, . . .) are known to be in the same proportion as in the population as a whole. Explain why we can't count on that method to give us a representative sample.

8.   One of my students was a blackjack dealer at a casino and heard a player say: "I ran a computer simulation of this system 1000 times and made money. So why didn't I win today playing for real?" Can you explain it?

9.   Is every randomly chosen sample representative? Explain.

Name _____ Section _____

Exercises for Section B

1. Your candidate is favored by 56% to 44%, with a margin of error of 5% and a confidence level of 94%. What does that mean?

2. You read a poll that says the confidence level is 71%. Is the generalization reliable?

3. a. What do we call a weak generalization from a sample that is obviously too small?

   b. Can a sample of one ever be enough for a strong generalization?

4. The larger the _____ in the population, the larger the sample size must be.

5. What premises do we need for a good generalization?

6. a. You're at the supermarket trying to decide which quart basket of strawberries to buy. Describe your procedure as a sampling and generalizing process. (Of course you can't actually taste one.)

   b. Now do the same supposing the basket is covered everywhere but on top.

7. The mayor of a town of 8,000 has to decide whether to spend town funds on renovating the park or hiring a part-time pest exterminator. He gets a reputable polling organization to do a survey.

    a. The results of the survey are 52% in favor of hiring a pest exterminator and 47% in favor of renovating the park, with 1% undecided, and a margin of error of 3%. The confidence level is 98%. Which choice will make the most people happy? Should he bet on that?

    b. The results are 68% in favor of hiring a pest exterminator and 24% in favor of renovating the park, with 8% undecided, and a margin of error of 9%. The confidence level is 94%. Which choice will make the most people happy? Should he bet on that?

8. Suppose you're on the city council and have to decide whether to put a bond issue for a new school on the next ballot. You don't want to do it if there's a good chance it will fail. You decide to do a survey, but haven't time to get a polling agency to do it. There are 7,200 people in your town. How would you go about picking a sample?

9. The president of your college would like to know how many students approve of the way she is handling her job. Explain why no survey is going to give her any useful ideas about how to improve her work.

10. You find a women's magazine in the doctor's waiting-room that has the results of a survey they've done on women's attitudes towards men with beards. They print the questions they asked in the last issue and say that they received over 10,000 responses from their readers, with 78% saying that they think that men with beards are really sexy. Should you tell your brother to grow a beard to improve his chances of getting a date?

11.

I TALKED TO ALL THE PEOPLE WHO LIVE ON THIS STREET AND EVERYONE WHO HAS A DOG IS REALLY HAPPY. SO IF I GET MY MOM A DOG, SHE'LL BE HAPPY, TOO.

How should Dick explain to Flo that she's not reasoning well?

12. Suppose your friend tells you:

"Lanolin is great for your hands—you ought to try it. It's what's on sheep wool naturally. How many shepherds have you seen with dry, chapped hands?"

What's the first question you should ask?

13. Dr. E was born. Therefore, Dr. E will die.
 a. What generalization is needed to make this a good argument?

 b. What is the sample?

 c. What is the population?

Explain what's wrong with the following two uses of general claims.

14. Most great men are dead. The author of this book is a great man. Therefore, the author of this book is dead.

15. (Ad on Southern California radio station) Cadillac is the most popular selling luxury car in Southern California. (Unstated conclusion) So you should get a Cadillac.

Below are a few of Tom's attempts to use the ideas of this chapter.

Maria: Every time I've seen a stranger come to Dick's gate, Spot has barked. So Spot will always bark at strangers at Dick's gate.

Generalization (state it; if none, say so) Spot will bark at every stranger who comes to the gate.

Sample: All the times Maria has seen a stranger come to the gate.

Sample is representative? (yes or no, with explanation) Who knows?

Sample is big enough? (yes or no) No.

Sample is studied well? (yes or no) Yes—Maria knows if Spot barked when she was there.

Additional premises needed:

Good generalization? No. The sample isn't good.

You almost got it. The generalization shouldn't convince you—that's right. But the problem isn't that the sample isn't "good," but that Maria hasn't given any reason to believe that it's big enough and representative. Is "every time" once? Twice? 150 times? And are those times representative? It's enough that you have no reason to believe that the sample is representative to make this a bad generalization, i.e., a bad argument.

In a study of 5,000 people who owned pets in Anchorage, Alaska, dog owners expressed higher satisfaction with their pets and their lives. So dog owners are more satisfied with their pets and their own lives.

Generalization (state it; if none, say so) Dog owners are more satisfied with their pets and their own lives.

Sample: The people surveyed.

Sample is representative? (yes or no, with explanation) No.

Sample is big enough? (yes or no) Don't know.

Sample is studied well? (yes or no) Not sure—I don't know what questions were asked.

Additional premises needed:

Good generalization? No. The sample isn't good.

Right. Once you note that the sample isn't representative, you know immediately that the argument isn't good.

Every time the minimum wage is raised, there's squawking that it will cause inflation and decrease employment. And every time it doesn't. So watch for the same worthless arguments again this time.

Generalization (state it; if none, say so) Raising the minimum wage won't cause inflation and decrease employment.

Sample: Every time in the past that the minimum wage was raised.

Sample is representative? (yes or no, with explanation) Yes.

Sample is big enough? (yes or no) Yes—it was all the times before.

Sample is studied well? (yes or no) Yes—assuming the speaker knows what she's talking about.

Additional premises needed: None.

Good generalization? Yes.

The sample is big enough, since it can't get any bigger. But is it representative? Is there any reason to think that the situation now is like the situations in the past when the minimum wage was raised? It's like an analogy: This time is like the past times. Until the speaker fills that in, we shouldn't accept the conclusion.

Maria has asked all but three of the thirty-six people in her class whether they've every used heroin. Only two said "yes." So Maria concludes that almost no one in the class has used heroin.

Generalization Almost no one in Maria's class has used heroin.

Sample: The thirty-four people Maria asked.

Sample is representative? Yes.

Sample is big enough? Yes.

Sample is studied well? (yes or no) Yes.

Additional premises needed:

Good generalization? Yes.

Do you really think everyone who's used heroin is going to admit it to a stranger? The sample isn't studied well—you'd need anonymous responses at least. So the generalization isn't good.

Evaluate Exercises 16–32 by filling in after the italics.

16. It's incredible how much information they can put on a CD. I just bought one that contains a whole encyclopedia.

    Generalization (state it; if none, say so)

    Sample:

    Sample is representative? (yes or no, with explanation)

    Sample is big enough? (yes or no)

    Sample is studied well? (yes or no)

    Additional premises needed:

    Good generalization?

17. Don't take a course from Dr. E. I know three people who failed his course last term.

Generalization (state it; if none, say so)

Sample:

Sample is representative? (yes or no, with explanation)

Sample is big enough? (yes or no)

Sample is studied well? (yes or no)

Additional premises needed:

Good generalization?

18. What's the IRS doing? It's always picking on us middle-class guys! Both my brother and I got audited this year.

Generalization (state it; if none, say so)

Sample:

Sample is representative? (yes or no, with explanation)

Sample is big enough? (yes or no)

Sample is studied well? (yes or no)

Additional premises needed:

Good generalization?

19. (At a health-food store)
    Customer: Have you got anything for this flu?
    Owner: Try this herbal tea. Everyone who's tried it here says it helped
              with the coughing.

Generalization (state it; if none, say so)

Sample:
Sample is representative? (yes or no, with explanation)

Sample is big enough? (yes or no)

Sample is studied well? (yes or no)

Additional premises needed:

Good generalization?

20. Everyone I've met at this college is either on one of the athletic teams or has a boy-friend or girlfriend on one of the athletic teams. Gosh, I guess just about everyone at this college is involved in sports.

    Generalization (state it; if none, say so)

    Sample:

    Sample is representative? (yes or no, with explanation)

    Sample is big enough? (yes or no)

    Sample is studied well? (yes or no)

    Additional premises needed:

    Good generalization?

21. Dick: Hold the steering wheel.
    Zoe: What are you doing? Stop! Are you crazy?
    Dick: I'm just taking my sweater off.
    Zoe: My Dog, I can't believe you did that. It's *so* dangerous.
    Dick: Don't be silly. I've done it a thousand times before.

    Generalization (state it; if none, say so)

    Sample:

    Sample is representative? (yes or no, with explanation)

    Sample is big enough? (yes or no)

    Sample is studied well? (yes or no)

    Additional premises needed:

    Good generalization?

22. My grandmother was diagnosed with cancer seven years ago. She refused any treatment that was offered to her over the years. She's perfectly healthy and doing great. The treatment for cancer is just a scam to get people's money.

    Generalization (state it; if none, say so)

    Sample:

    Sample is representative? (yes or no, with explanation)

    Sample is big enough? (yes or no)

    Sample is studied well? (yes or no)

    Additional premises needed:

    Good generalization?

23. Maria goes out with two bald men and decides that she'll date only bald men in the future, they're so sexy.

    Generalization (state it; if none, say so)

    Sample:

    Sample is representative? (yes or no, with explanation)

    Sample is big enough? (yes or no)

    Sample is studied well? (yes or no)

    Additional premises needed:

    Good generalization?

24. Maria goes out with two men who smoke and decides that she won't date men who smoke anymore because their breath smells like old ashtrays.

    Generalization (state it; if none, say so)

    Sample:

    Sample is representative? (yes or no, with explanation)

Sample is big enough? (yes or no)

Sample is studied well? (yes or no)

Additional premises needed:

Good generalization?

25. Tom: Can you pick up that pro basketball player who's coming to the rally today?
    Dick: I can't. Zoe's got the car. Why not ask Suzy?
    Tom: She's got one of those compact Yodas. They're too small for someone over 6'4".
    Generalization (state it; if none, say so)

    Sample:
    Sample is representative? (yes or no, with explanation)

    Sample is big enough? (yes or no)

    Sample is studied well? (yes or no)

    Additional premises needed:

    Good generalization?

26. Give the baby his pacifier so he'll stop crying. Every time I give him the pacifier he stops crying.
    Generalization (state it; if none, say so)

    Sample:
    Sample is representative? (yes or no, with explanation)

    Sample is big enough? (yes or no)

    Sample is studied well? (yes or no)

    Additional premises needed:

    Good generalization?

27. (Overheard at a doctor's office)
    I won't have high blood pressure today because I got enough sleep last night. The last two times you've taken my blood pressure I've rested well the night before and both times it was normal.
    Generalization (state it; if none, say so)

    Sample:

    Sample is representative? (yes or no, with explanation)

    Sample is big enough? (yes or no)

    Sample is studied well? (yes or no)

    Additional premises needed:

    Good generalization?

28. We will be late for church because we have to wait for Gina. She's always late. She's been late seven Sundays in a row.
    Generalization (state it; if none, say so)

    Sample:
    Sample is representative? (yes or no, with explanation)

    Sample is big enough? (yes or no)

    Sample is studied well? (yes or no)

    Additional premises needed:

    Good generalization?

29. Gina will be at Club Rio Friday night. She's been going there every Friday night since it opened two months ago.
    Generalization (state it; if none, say so)

    Sample:

Sample is representative? (yes or no, with explanation)

Sample is big enough? (yes or no)

Sample is studied well? (yes or no)

Additional premises needed:

Good generalization?

30. Maria: I've been searching for jobs on the Internet by description. I didn't look at any jobs called "sales associate" or "sales," because all the sales jobs I've had before didn't work out or I didn't like them.

    Generalization (state it; if none, say so)

    Sample:
    Sample is representative? (yes or no, with explanation)

    Sample is big enough? (yes or no)

    Sample is studied well? (yes or no)

    Additional premises needed:

    Good generalization?

31. **Biology breeds grumpy old men**
    Men lose brain tissue at almost three times the rate of women, curbing their memory, concentration and reasoning power—and perhaps turning them into "grumpy old men" —a researcher said Wednesday.
    "Even in the age range of 18 to 45, you can see a steady decline in the ability to perform such (attention-oriented) tasks in men," said Ruben C. Gur, a professor of psychology at the University of Pennsylvania.
    Gur said shrinking brains may make men grumpier because some of the tissue loss is in the left frontal region of the brain, which seems to be connected to depression.
    "Grumpy old men may be biological," said Gur, who is continuing to study whether there is a connection.
    However, one researcher not affiliated with the study said Wednesday that other recent studies contradict Gur's findings on shrinkage.

The findings, which augment earlier research published by Gur and colleagues, are the result of his studies of the brain functions of 24 women and 37 men over the past decade. He measured the brain volume with an MRI machine and studied metabolism rates. From young adulthood to middle age, men lose 15% of their frontal lobe volume, 8.5% of temporal lobe, he said. Women, while they have "very mild" shrinkage, lose tissue in neither lobe. For the brain overall, men lose tissue three times faster.

Gur found that the most dramatic loss was in men's frontal lobes, which control attention, abstract reasoning, mental flexibility and inhibition of impulses, and the temporal lobe [which] governs memory.   Associated Press, April, 1996

Generalization (state it; if none, say so)

Sample:

Sample is representative? (yes or no, with explanation)

Sample is big enough? (yes or no)

Sample is studied well? (yes or no)

Additional premises needed:

Good generalization?

32. **Sex unlikely to cause heart attacks**
Sexual intercourse is unlikely to trigger a heart attack, even among people who have already survived one, according to a study that is the first to examine this widespread fear.

Only 1 percent of heart attacks were triggered by sexual activity in a nationwide sample of nearly 900 heart attack survivors who said they were sexually active.

The odds of suffering a heart attack after engaging in sex are only about 2 in a million, the study found—about twice as high as the average hourly risk of heart attack among 50-year-old Americans with no overt sign of coronary artery disease.

"It's easy to get the message from movies, and even from Shakespeare, that sexual activity can trigger heart attacks," said Dr. James Muller of New England Deaconess Hospital in Boston, who led the study. "It's part of the mythology, and it's certainly in the minds of many cardiac patients and their spouses."

"What has been lacking in the past are actual numbers. Now the numbers are available, and the risk is quite, quite low."

Furthermore, regular exercise can substantially reduce the risk of a sex-triggered heart attack.

Patients who never engaged in heavy physical exertion, or got vigorous exercise only once a week, had a threefold risk of heart attack in the two hours after sexual activity. But the relative risk dropped to twofold among patients who exercise twice a week, and only 1.2 fold among those who exercised three or more times weekly.

The new figures, which appear in this week's Journal of the American Medical Association, suggest that sexual activity triggers 15,000 of the 1.5 million heart attacks that occur in this nation annually.

"Although sexual activity doubles the risk" of heart attack, the researchers noted, the effect on annual risk "is negligible because the absolute risk difference is small, the risk is transient and the activity is relatively infrequent."

For instance, for an individual without cardiac disease, weekly sexual activity would increase the annual risk of a heart attack from 1 percent to 1.01 percent.

Richard Knox, *Boston Globe,* May 8, 1996

Generalization (state it; if none, say so)

Sample:

Sample is representative? (yes or no, with explanation)

Sample is big enough? (yes or no)

Sample is studied well? (yes or no)

Additional premises needed:

Good generalization?

33. Would you try this new procedure? Explain.

Chili peppers a red hot cure for surgical pain

When burning pain lingers months after surgery, doctors say there is a red-hot cure: chili peppers.

In a study, an ointment made with capsaicin, the stuff that makes chili peppers hot, brought relief to patients with tender surgical scars, apparently by short-circuiting the pain.

Patients undergoing major cancer surgery, such as mastectomies or lung operations, are sometimes beset by sharp, burning pain in their surgical scars that lasts for months, even years. Sometimes the misery is so bad that sufferers cannot even stand the weight of clothing on their scar, even though it is fully healed.

The condition, seen in about 5 percent or fewer of all cases, results from damage to the nerves during surgery. Ordinary pain killers don't work, and the standard treatment is antidepressant drugs.

However, these powerful drugs have side effects. So in search of a better alternative, doctors tested a cream made with capsaicin on 99 patients who typically had suffered painful surgical scars at least six months.

Patients preferred capsaicin over a dummy cream by 3-to-1.

"The therapy clearly worked," said Dr. Charles L. Loprinzi, head of medical oncology at the Mayo Clinic. He released his data Monday at the annual meeting of the American Society for Clinical Oncology.

Capsaicin is believed to work by blocking substance P, a natural chemical that carries pain impulses between nerve cells. That same blocking effect may explain why people who eat hot peppers all the time develop a tolerance to the burn.

Dr. Alan Lyss of Missouri Baptist Medical Center in St. Louis called it "a creative, new and very inexpensive way to take care of some kinds of cancer pain."

Capsaicin is sold in drug stores without a prescription, and a tube that lasts a month costs about $16. . . .

In the study, the patients were randomly assigned to capsaicin cream or the look-alike placebo four times a day for eight-week intervals. Until the study was over, no one knew which was which.

Patients kept score of their pain. It went down 53 percent while using capsaicin but only 17 percent while on the placebo. About 10 percent said their pain disappeared completely.

The doctors followed the patients for two months after they stopped using capsaicin and found that pain did not come back. Longer follow-up will be necessary to see if the treatment relieves the pain permanently. . . .

Associated Press, May 21, 1996

For Exercises 34 and 35, identify the analogy and explain how a generalization is required.

34. Dick: What do you think about buying a Yoda sedan?
    Zoe: It's not a good idea. Remember, Suzy got a Yoda and she's had trouble with it from day one.

35. Of chimpanzees fed one pound of chocolate per day in addition to their usual diet, 72% became obese within two months. Therefore, it is likely that most humans who eat 2% of their body weight in chocolate daily will become obese within two months.

15   Cause and Effect

Key Words

causal claim	reversed cause and effect
cause	common cause
effect	*post hoc, ergo propter hoc*
normal conditions	coincidence
particular cause and effect	cause in populations
general cause and effect	control group
perfect correlation	common thread
foreseeable consequence	controlled cause-to-effect experiment
intervening cause	uncontrolled cause-to-effect experiment
	uncontrolled effect-to-cause experiment

Exercises for Sections A.1–A.3

For each of the following sentences, if appropriate rewrite it as a claim that uses the word "causes" or "caused." If it's a *particular* causal claim, state the cause and the effect as claims. Here are two of Tom's homeworks.

Your teaching made me fail this class.

Causal claim: Your teaching caused me to fail this class.
Particular or *general*? Particular.
Cause (stated as a claim): You taught badly.
Effect (stated as a claim): I failed.

You've got the idea. But why did you say the cause was "You taught badly"? Maybe it should be "You taught well, but didn't slow down for unprepared students." The problem is that the original sentence is <u>too vague</u>.

Drinking coffee keeps people awake.

Causal claim: Drinking coffee causes people to stay awake.
Particular or *general*? General.
Cause (stated as a claim): People drink coffee.
Effect (stated as a claim): People stay awake.

O.K., but remember that with a general causal claim there isn't a cause and effect, but lots of them. So there's no point in filling in after "cause" and "effect." When we try to figure out a particular causal claim that this general one covers, we see the real problem: Maria drank coffee yesterday, Maria stayed awake. How long did she stay awake? What would count for making this true? It's still too vague.

1. The police car's siren got me to pull over.

    Causal claim:

    Particular or *general*?

    Cause (stated as a claim):

    Effect (stated as a claim):

2. You doing so badly in this class made me teach badly.

    Causal claim:

    Particular or *general*?

    Cause (stated as a claim):

    Effect (stated as a claim):

3. Because you were late, we missed the beginning of the movie.

    Causal claim:

    Particular or *general*?

    Cause (stated as a claim):

    Effect (stated as a claim):

4. Dogs make great pets.

    Causal claim:

    Particular or *general*?

    Cause (stated as a claim):

    Effect (stated as a claim):

5. I'd better not get the pizza with anchovies, because every time I do, I get heartburn.

    Causal claim:

    Particular or *general*?

    Cause (stated as a claim):

    Effect (stated as a claim):

6. I would have passed the exam if Dr. E hadn't collected the papers five minutes early.

   Causal claim:

   Particular or *general*?

   Cause (stated as a claim):

   Effect (stated as a claim):

7. You allowing me to take the final exam a day early made it possible for me to pass.

   Causal claim:

   Particular or *general*?

   Cause (stated as a claim):

   Effect (stated as a claim):

8. Watching golf makes me want to play golf.

   Causal claim:

   Particular or *general*?

   Cause (stated as a claim):

   Effect (stated as a claim):

9. Penicillin prevents serious infection.

   Causal claim:

   Particular or *general*?

   Cause (stated as a claim):

   Effect (stated as a claim):

10. If it weren't for my boyfriend, I'd have no problems.

    Causal claim:

    Particular or *general*?

    Cause (stated as a claim):

    Effect (stated as a claim):

11. Because of religion, people act more virtuously.

    Causal claim:

    Particular or *general*?

    Cause (stated as a claim):

    Effect (stated as a claim):

12. The result of watching too much TV is lessened intelligence.

   Causal claim:

   Particular or *general*?

   Cause (stated as a claim):

   Effect (stated as a claim):

13. Our airplane took off from gate number thirteen. No wonder we're experiencing so much turbulence.

   Causal claim:

   Particular or *general*?

   Cause (stated as a claim):

   Effect (stated as a claim):

14. Your big mouth led to my getting fired.

   Causal claim:

   Particular or *general*?

   Cause (stated as a claim):

   Effect (stated as a claim):

15. The garage being under my bedroom makes my room hotter than the rest of the house.

   Causal claim:

   Particular or *general*?

   Cause (stated as a claim):

   Effect (stated as a claim):

16. Being cold causes people to shiver.

   Causal claim:

   Particular or *general*?

   Cause (stated as a claim):

   Effect (stated as a claim):

17. Zoe made me lose my virginity.

   Causal claim:

   Particular or *general*?

   Cause (stated as a claim):

   Effect (stated as a claim):

Exercises for Sections A and B

1. What criteria are necessary for there to be cause and effect?

2. What criteria do we know are sufficient for there to be cause and effect?

3. Why isn't a perfect correlation enough to justify cause and effect? Explain.

4. Comparable to the unstated premises of an argument, what do we call the claims that must be true for a causal claim to be true?

Here's some of Tom's work on cause and effect. He's supposed to fill in after the italics and explain why the causal claim is plausible or clearly wrong.

> **I used Diabolic Grow on my plants and they grew great! I'll always use it.**
>
> *Causal claim*: (unstated) Diabolic Grow caused my plants to grow great.
>
> *Cause*: The speaker put Diabolic Grow on his plants.
>
> *Effect*: The plants grew great.
>
> *Cause before and close in space and time to effect*? Apparently so.
>
> *Cause makes a difference*? It seems so, but did the cause really make a difference? Maybe they would have grown great anyway. Some years that happens when it rains at just the right time in the spring.
>
> *Evaluation*: You'd need a lot more evidence to believe the claim.
>
> *Excellent! You're thinking critically.*

For each of Exercises 5–16 isolate the causal claim. Then evaluate it, explaining why it's plausible or clearly wrong.

5. Our airplane took off from gate number thirteen. No wonder we're experiencing so much turbulence.

    Causal claim:

    Cause:

    Effect:

    Cause before and close in space and time to effect?

    Cause makes a difference?

    Evaluation:

6. Dick: Ooh, my stomach hurts.
    Zoe: Serves you right. You really pigged out on the nachos and salsa last night.
           They always give you a stomach ache.

    Causal claim:

    Cause:

    Effect:

    Cause before and close in space and time to effect?

    Cause makes a difference?

    Evaluation:

7. Zoe: This is horrible. My license was revoked!
    Dick: That's what you get for driving after you drank so much.

    Causal claim:

    Cause:

    Effect:

    Cause before and close in space and time to effect?

    Cause makes a difference?

    Evaluation:

8. Suzy: I'm really depressed today because of the dark sky.

    Causal claim:

    Cause:

    Effect:

    Cause before and close in space and time to effect?

    Cause makes a difference?

    Evaluation:

9. Marriage is the chief cause of divorce.

   Causal claim:

   Cause:

   Effect:

   Cause before and close in space and time to effect?

   Cause makes a difference?

   Evaluation:

10. (OSHA booklet, "Safety with Beef Cattle")
    Hazards are one of the main causes of accidents.

    Causal claim:

    Cause:

    Effect:

    Cause before and close in space and time to effect?

    Cause makes a difference?

    Evaluation:

11. Zoe: We've run out of gas.
    Dick: It's 'cause you forgot to fill up before we left town.

    Causal claim:

    Cause:

    Effect:

    Cause before and close in space and time to effect?

    Cause makes a difference?

    Evaluation:

12. The emphasis on Hollywood figures in the media causes people to use drugs, because people want to emulate the stars.

    Causal claim:

    Cause:

    Effect:

    Cause before and close in space and time to effect?

    Cause makes a difference?

    Evaluation:

13. My instructor's high standards make me work hard in this class.

    Causal claim:

    Cause:

    Effect:

    Cause before and close in space and time to effect?

    Cause makes a difference?

    Evaluation:

14. Harry's college education helped him get a high-paying job the year after he graduated.

    Causal claim:

    Cause:

    Effect:

    Cause before and close in space and time to effect?

    Cause makes a difference?

    Evaluation:

15. Dick: Every day I run up this hill and it's no big deal. Why am I so beat today?

    Zoe: It's 'cause you stayed out late and didn't get enough sleep.

    Causal claim:

    Cause:

    Effect:

    Cause before and close in space and time to effect?

    Cause makes a difference?

    Evaluation:

16. Zoe: My life's a mess. I've never really been happy since all those years ago in high school you told Sally that I killed Puff. She believed your stupid joke, and made sure I wasn't a cheerleader. I'll never be a cheerleader. It's your fault I'm so miserable now.

    Dick: There, there.

    Causal claim:

    Cause:

    Effect:

    Cause before and close in space and time to effect?

    Cause makes a difference?

    Evaluation:

17. Make up five causal claims and trade with a classmate to analyze.

   a.

   b.

   c.

   d.

   e.

18. Judge: I find that Nancy sustained serious injuries in this accident. There is sufficient evidence that the defendant ran a red light and broadsided her car, causing the injuries. But I hold that Nancy was partly responsible for the severity of her injuries in that she was not wearing a seatbelt. Therefore, Nancy shall collect only 50% of the costs associated with this accident.

Explain the judge's decision in terms of normal conditions and foreseeable consequences.

19. Mickey has taken his four-wheel-drive jeep out into the desert to explore on this hot sunny Sunday. But his two cousins want to see him dead. Bertha has put poison in Mickey's five-gallon canteen. Richard, not knowing of Bertha's plans, has put a very small hole in the canteen.

Mickey's car breaks down. He's getting hot and thirsty. His cellular phone doesn't work because he forgot to recharge it. He goes to get some water and finds the canteen empty . . . *music swells*

Overcome by guilt later in the year, both Bertha and Richard confess. Who should be blamed for causing Mickey's death by thirst?

Exercises for Section C

For Exercises 1–4, come up with a method to determine whether there's cause and effect.

1. Pressing the "Door Close" button in the elevator causes the doors to close.

2. Zoe's belching caused Spot to run away.

3. The red-head walking by the classroom causes Professor Zzzyzzx to arrive at class on time.

4. Reducing the speed limit to 55 m.p.h. saves lives.

5. When should we trust authorities rather than figure out a cause for ourselves?

6. Explain: The way to answer a charge of *post hoc ergo propter hoc* is to show that the purported cause does make a difference.

7. Explain why a *post hoc* argument is just a bad generalization.

8. Explain why it's not amazing that every day a few dream predictions come true.

Tom was asked to bring in a causal claim he made recently and evaluate it. Here's his work:

The only time I've had a really bad backache is right after I went bicycling early in the morning when it was so cold last week. Bicycling never bothered me before. So it must be the cold weather that caused my back to hurt after cycling.

Causal claim: The cold weather caused my back to hurt after cycling.

Cause: It was cold when I went cycling.

Effect: I got a backache.

Evaluation (Criteria satisfied? Common mistake? How could you determine if true?):
The criteria seem to be satisfied. But now I'm wondering if I haven't overlooked some other cause. I also had an upset stomach. So maybe it was the flu. Or maybe it was tension, since I'd had a fight with Suzy the night before. I guess I'll have to try cycling in the cold again to find out.

Good. But you're still looking for <u>the</u> cause, when it may be <u>a</u> cause. Another possible cause: Did you warm up first? Another possibility: You'll never know for sure.

9. Write down a causal claim that you made recently and evaluate it like Tom's example. Have a classmate critique your evaluation.

Evaluate Exercises 10–22 in the same way that Tom did above.

10. Dick: (*Bending over, sweating and cursing*) There's something wrong with my bike.
    Zoe: What?
    Dick: Something's going "click," "click," "click" all the time.
    Zoe: Must be something that's moving.
    Dick: Duh. Here, hold it up while I turn the pedals. *click, click, click, . . .*
    Zoe: Yup, there it is.
    Dick: It must be in the pedals or the wheels.
    Zoe: Stop pedaling. . . . It's gone away.
    Dick: It must be in the pedals, then.
    Causal claim:

    Cause:

    Effect:

    Evaluation (Criteria satisfied? Common mistake? How could you determine if true?):

11. Sex, drugs, and rock 'n roll are the causes of the decline in family values.
    Causal claim:

    Cause:

    Effect:

    Evaluation (Criteria satisfied? Common mistake? How could you determine if true?):

12. I've got to go to the game. The only time I wasn't in the bleachers this season, they lost.
    Causal claim:

    Cause:

    Effect:

    Evaluation (Criteria satisfied? Common mistake? How could you determine if true?):

13. Just look at all the sex and violence on TV. That's why we're such a violent society.
    Causal claim:

    Cause:

    Effect:

    Evaluation (Criteria satisfied? Common mistake? How could you determine if true?):

14.

ISN'T IT AMAZING THAT OF ALL THE HOUSES IN THIS TOWN, I WAS BORN IN ONE WHERE THE PEOPLE LOOK SO MUCH LIKE ME !

What is Flo overlooking?

15. My neighbor said it's been the worst season ever for allergies this spring, but I told her I hadn't had any bad days. Then today I started sneezing. Darn it—if only she hadn't told me.

Causal claim:

Cause:

Effect:

Evaluation (Criteria satisfied? Common mistake? How could you determine if true?):

16. Dick: Normally my pulse rate is about 130 after exercising on this bike.

Zoe: I can't believe you actually measure your heart rate! You're so obsessive.

Dick: But for the past week or so it's been about 105. That's odd.

Zoe: You stopped drinking coffee two weeks ago, remember?

Causal claim:

Cause:

Effect:

Evaluation (Criteria satisfied? Common mistake? How could you determine if true?):

17. Satan causes evil.

Causal claim:

Cause:

Effect:

Evaluation (Criteria satisfied? Common mistake? How could you determine if true?):

18. He's stupid because his mother dropped him on his head when he was young.

    Causal claim:

    Cause:

    Effect:

    Evaluation (Criteria satisfied? Common mistake? How could you determine if true?):

19. Grey clouds cause rain.

    Causal claim:

    Cause:

    Effect:

    Evaluation (Criteria satisfied? Common mistake? How could you determine if true?):

20. (From a public service ad)

    Untreated depression is the #1 cause of suicide.

    Causal claim:

    Cause:

    Effect:

    Evaluation (Criteria satisfied? Common mistake? How could you determine if true?):

21. A recent study showed that everyone who uses heroin started with marijuana.
    So smoking marijuana causes heroin use.

    Causal claim:

    Cause:

    Effect:

    Evaluation (Criteria satisfied? Common mistake? How could you determine if true?):

22. Dr. E: My students don't like the material at the end of this course. That's why so many
    have missed class the last two weeks of the course.

    Causal claim:

    Cause:

    Effect:

    Evaluation (Criteria satisfied? Common mistake? How could you determine if true?):

Pick out the cause and effect(s) here. Explain your answer.

Exercises for Section D

Describe what evidence you have for the claims in Exercises 1–5 and what experiments you would devise to try to prove or disprove them. [Don't do the experiments yourself! Some of them are dangerous without adult supervision.]

1. Universities cause students to become smarter.

2. Hedonistic life styles cause premature death.

3. Money brings happiness.

4. Drinking alcohol causes promiscuous behavior.

5. Unprotected sex causes disease.

6. **Study: Better primary care increases hospitalization**
   Researchers set out to show that giving sick people better access to family doctors keeps them out of the hospital. But to the surprise of everyone involved, the study found just the opposite.

Doctors apparently end up diagnosing more ills, including ones that probably would otherwise go unnoticed.

"I went in knowing that primary care could help keep these patients out of the hospital. That was my passion. I was exactly wrong," said Dr. Eugene Z. Oddone of the Veterans Affairs hospital in Durham, N.C.

He and Dr. Morris Weinberger of the VA hospital in Indianapolis had thought the experiment would prove the obvious: Better primary care keeps people healthier, reducing hospital admissions by about one-third and saving money.

Working with nine VA hospitals, they offered poor, seriously ill veterans the kind of care available in most HMOs—ready access to a nurse, a family doctor in charge of their case, reminders of appointments and follow-up calls.

After six months of this attention, hospitalizations actually rose by one-third.

"We were more surprised than anybody," Weinberger said.

The doctors said their study, published in Thursday's issue of the New England Journal of Medicine, illustrates one of the difficulties of refashioning the health care system: Even common-sense ideas need to be tested to make sure they work.

Furthermore, for some, it raises doubts about an article of faith among doctors— that catching and treating diseases early will make people healthier in the long run.

In an accompanying editorial, Dr. H. Gilbert Welch of Dartmouth Medical School said the study forces doctors to consider a "heretical view."

"Instead of conferring benefit, closer scrutiny of the patients simply led to more medical care and perhaps to harm," he said. "We can no longer assume that early intervention is always the right thing to do."

Associated Press, May 30, 1996

a. What causal claim is at issue?

b. Which type of causation-in-population experiment was done?

c. Evaluate whether it looks like it was done well.

d. How would you further test the claim?

7. **Saliva may spread deadly virus**
A virus linked to skin cancer occurring in many AIDS patients may be spread by saliva, University of Washington scientists say.

The virus KSHV, which is linked to the cancer Kaposi's sarcoma, does not cause AIDS, but it probably must be present for the cancer to occur.

The University of Washington researchers found it in the saliva of 17 out of 23 men who had both the cancer and the AIDS-causing HIV (human immuno-deficiency virus), which makes the body more susceptible to many diseases.

"It (KSHV) may be capable of spreading to others by saliva contact," said David Koelle, a University of Washington assistant professor of medicine who presented his team's research findings in New Orleans this week at the 36th Interscience Conference on Antimicrobial Agents and Chemotherapy.

KSHV was first identified in 1994. Up to one-third of HIV-infected gay or bisexual men develop Kaposi's sarcoma before death. They may carry KSHV for some time before the body's immune system becomes weak and susceptible to the cancer.

The cancer is not found in patients who were infected with HIV exclusively through blood—injection drug users, hemophiliacs or transfusion recipients. Kaposi's sarcoma commonly spreads to the gastrointestinal tract or lungs, causing death.

The University of Washington scientists also found KSHV in two gay men who had HIV but not Kaposi's sarcoma, and in one patient who had Kaposi's sarcoma but not HIV. They did not find it in any of the 24 heterosexual adults who were not infected with HIV.

Outside of HIV patients, Kaposi's sarcoma is rare. But it also occurs in men without HIV, especially elderly men in southern Europe, and in Africa, both in adults and as an aggressive form in infants.

Koelle said KHSV is genetically similar to the Epstein-Barr virus, which is spread by saliva and causes infectious mononucleosis, with symptoms of fatigue, fever and swollen lymph nodes.

"While the relationship between KSHV infection and Kaposi's sarcoma has not been formally proven, it is highly likely that infection with the virus is required for development of the disease," Koelle said.

Koelle said more research needs to be conducted on KSHV.

Seattle Times, September 19, 1996

a.   What is the argument here?

b.   What experiment was done?

c.   Explain whether the experiment proves the claim.

8. **Vitamin E in moderation may protect heart**

Eating a moderate amount of food rich in vitamin E, such as nuts, vegetable oils and margarine, reduces the risk of death from heart disease, says a study in today's New England Journal of Medicine.

This supports a growing body of evidence that links vitamin E to a healthy heart.

Researchers surveyed 34,486 postmenopausal women about their eating habits in

1986 and followed up about seven years later. They studied women but say the results apply to men, too.

They found women with the diets highest in vitamin E-rich foods had half the risk of death from heart disease compared with those eating diets low in these foods. The highest group got more than 10 IUs of vitamin E from food daily, the equivalent of about an ounce of almonds. Those in the lowest group got about half that amount.

Margarine and salad dressings are high in fat and calories, so people should use common sense when eating them. "I wouldn't go overboard with these things, but I wouldn't necessarily cut them out entirely," says the study's lead author, Lawrence H. Kushi of the University of Minnesota School of Public Health. The women who did the best in the research did not eat "outrageous amounts" of vitamin E foods.

Dr. Walter Willett, Harvard School of Public Health, says "one of the unfortunate parts of the fat phobia is that people eliminate major sources of vitamin E in their diets."

This study didn't come to a definitive conclusion on supplements, but other studies indicate they are beneficial.

Other rich sources of vitamin E: hazelnuts, sunflower seeds, wheat germ, mayonnaise, peanut butter, avocados.

Nanci Hellmich, *USA TODAY,* 1996

a.   What causal claim is at issue?

b.   Which type of causation-in-population experiment was done?

c.   Evaluate whether it looks like it was done well.

d.   How would you further test the claim?

9.   **Every breath you take**
     It's not muscles alone that get you up the road. Breathing supplies the oxygen that makes those well-trained quads work. But many cyclists can't control the simple act of respiration. They don't know how to breathe efficiently, and they waste energy and gasp uncomfortably on climbs.

     At the bike camps in Colorado where I'm an instructor, many campers fly in from sea level and the next day they're laboring up Tennessee Pass at 10,000 feet, gasping like beached fish. That's when I ride alongside and explain how to get the most out of every breath. This approach, called "switchside breathing," produces almost miraculous increases in climbing speed and comfort—and it's easy to learn. I picked it up from Ian Jackson, author of the book *BreathPlay,* when we used to go snowshoe running around Aspen. Then I started to use it on the bike.

No one is quite sure why switchside breathing helps. When I was a mountain runner, I noticed that a runner's injuries would often be on the same side. For example, his right knee, ankle and hamstrung all hurt. And the injuries often coincided with his dominant breathing side. But when we taught him to switchside breathe, the injuries went away. Apparently, if you always breathe on one side, you may subconsciously exert more force on that side. Switchside breathing balances out the effort of the legs and makes climbing easier. Give it a try!

Start by practicing correct athletic breathing off the bike. Lie on your back on the floor with a book on your stomach. Breathe in slowly and fully, expanding your diaphragm, not your chest. The book should move toward the ceiling. Then exhale steadily so it moves down toward the floor.

Most people think they should expand their chests, as a drill sergeant does. But if you look at side view photos of professional riders like Miguel Indurain or Tony Rominger, they almost look fat. Their diaphragms are expanded like bullfrogs in full voice. It may look funny—but it leaves more room for air to get into your lungs.

Now try it on the bike. Most riders exhale, every time, on the same side of the pedal stroke. If you're right-handed, you probably breathe out when the right pedal starts the downstroke. You can check by climbing a flight of stairs and paying attention to your pattern of in- and out-breaths. Once you get a rhythm going, I bet you exhale each time the same foot hits a step.

The easiest way to break out of this pattern of same-side breathing is simply to take an extra-long out-breath every five to ten pedal strokes. That will automatically switch your out-breath to the other down-stroke. Try it a couple of times on long climbs and it will become second nature. You can even practice off the bike by climbing stairs in a tall building. While stair climbing, the footstrike is slower and more pronounced, so it's easier to coordinate with breathing.

Finally, emphasize the out-breath. If you force air out of your mouth, you won't even need to think about breathing in. It will happen automatically. Some riders make a guttural sound as they breathe out, like weight lifters. Ex-pro Davis Phinney jokes about sounding like a pen full of pigs when we climb, but it works.

Skip Hamilton, *Bicycling,* June, 1997

a. What causal claim is at issue?

b. Which type of experiment was done?

c. Evaluate whether it looks like it was done well.

    d.   How would you further test the claim?

    e.   Would you use this technique yourself?

10. Letter to the editor:

In case you missed it, the cost of getting your car's air conditioner serviced shot up like a rocket this summer. Whereas just a few short years ago you could buy a pound of Freon for a dollar or two, today the price has climbed to more than $20 a pound. And why?

Because environmentalists have sold us a lie. They have told us that unless we get rid of the CFC's we use in our air conditioners and refrigerators, we will punch a hole in the ozone layer and fry like bacon from the sun's UV rays. But the facts don't support their doomsdayism.

For one thing, there has never been any decline in atmospheric ozone. As noted by Dr. Ken Towe of the Smithsonian Institute, NASA data over the past 40 years has shown no downward trend in ozone thickness—a direct refutation of the theory.

Secondly, there is no documented increase in UV-B radiation. In fact, as demonstrated by the UV monitoring network that existed in this country from the early 1970s to the mid-1980s, there has been a slight decrease in UV-B—exactly the opposite of what the theory maintains.

And finally, as for the so-called ozone hole over Antarctica, well, that was discovered by none other than Dr. Gordon Dobson, the "father" of modern atmospheric research, in 1956—years before CFCs came into widespread use!

So, remember who to thank when you receive an enormous bill to "fix" your car's air conditioning system this year.

                                   J. C. Marcelli, *Las Vegas Review-Journal*, 1996

    a.   What causal claim is at issue?

    b.   Evaluate the evidence for it.

11. **Prozac, pregnancy woes linked**

Women who take the widely prescribed anti-depressant Prozac in the final months of pregnancy may be doing harm to their babies, according to a new study.

California researchers followed hundreds of women taking the medicine, generically known as fluoxetine, during all stages of pregnancy and found that the risk of prematurity, admission to special-care nursery and poor outcome were more common in babies exposed to the drug in the last trimester.

But researchers from several laboratories caution that the study, to be published today in the New England Journal of Medicine, lacks the proper controls, and that the effects could be due to the mother's depression and not to the medication.

"I do not think that fluoxetine or tricyclic anti-depressant drugs have been clearly proved unsafe for pregnant women," Dr. Elisabeth Robert, a researcher at the Institut Europeen des Genomutations in France, wrote in an accompanying editorial. "It seems unjustified to use these new results as a reason to withhold fluoxetine from women who require an anti-depressant during pregnancy."

Christina Chambers and her colleagues at the California Teratogen Information Service and Clinical Research Program at the University of California, San Diego, studied 228 pregnant women taking fluoxetine, and compared the birth outcomes with another 254 women not taking the anti-depressant. Thirty percent of the women on Prozac were also taking another mind-altering medication.

According to the study, babies whose mothers took Prozac during the first trimester had no greater percentage of miscarriage, stillbirth or major birth defects than those unexposed to Prozac.

Among those mothers who continued to take Prozac, a drug that alters the brain chemical serotonin, well into the last trimester, there was a higher incidence of premature delivery and their babies were twice as likely to be placed in special-care nurseries. These babies were more jittery, suffered more respiratory problems and even the full-term babies were smaller than the comparison groups.

"Depressed women need to know what the risks might be so that they can discuss them with their doctors and be ready to deal with complications should they occur," Chambers said in an interview.

Dr. David Goldstein, clinical research physician at Eli Lilly, maker of Prozac, said the study did not control for the fact that depression itself has been associated with premature births and neonatal complications.

Patricia Whitaker-Azmitia, associate professor of psychiatry at the State University of New York at Stony Brook, has been studying the effects of Prozac and other anti-depressants on the developing animal in utero. Her animal studies have shown that serotonin, the major brain chemical altered by these drugs, is a key developmental hormone. Changes in the hormone during development of the central nervous system led to many problems in animals, she said. "They had learning deficits, were extremely aggressive and never formed social attachments. At birth, they were very much like the babies in this study, hyper-reactive and suffering from respiratory problems."

"To say not to worry is irresponsible," she said. On the other hand, there have been a handful of human studies that did not find any obvious physical problems of premature births in women exposed during the third trimester to antidepressants, Goldstein said. He worries that depressed women may prematurely decide to stop taking their medicine, and could suffer a rebound depression and hurt themselves.

Goldstein said that physicians should be as conservative as possible when prescribing any drug during pregnancy.

The March of Dimes Birth Defects Foundation recommends that pregnant women try to avoid taking the drug until its effects have been studied better. It added that pregnant women should not stop taking Prozac without first consulting their doctors.

Newsday, October 3, 1996

a. What causal claim is at issue?

b. Describe the experiment. What type is it?

c. What flaw in the experiment is described? Which of the mistakes in reasoning about causes does it fall under?

d. Devise a study that doesn't have that flaw. Would it be ethical to do?

e. How does risk factor into your evaluation of whether to advise pregnant women to stop taking Prozac? Relate that to the strength of the causal arguments.

Here are two pairs of arguments or descriptions of experiments for you to analyze. Each involves some causal claim. Prepare a full analysis of each in the style of the long argument analysis on pp. 239–241 of the text. They'll take all the skills you've learned in this course. They're long enough that you will need to use separate pages for them.

12. **Power lines and leukemia: beware of scientists bearing glad tidings**
     "No Adverse Health Effects Seen From Residential Exposure to Electromagnetic Fields," said the press release from the National Academy of Sciences (NAS). "Study Fails to Link EMFs With Illnesses," repeated the *Los Angeles Times*. "Panel Sees No Proof of Health Hazards From Power Lines," "Electromagnetic research review finds no danger," "Power lines cleared as cause of cancer," "Power Line Hazard Called Small," echoed the *New York Times, Boston Globe, San Francisco Examiner,* and *Washington Post.*

     Feel better now? No need to worry about buying or renting a home near high-voltage electric power lines. Forget the scare stories about your children getting leukemia (cancer of the blood), and worry about real problems like the kids being abducted by aliens.

     But the headlines lie. Digging a bit deeper reveals that the study issued last October by a panel of 16 distinguished experts does not exonerate power lines, nor electromagnetic fields (EMFs), from being a danger to human health. In fact, the report itself (as opposed to the press release) summarizes the many existing epidemiological studies as saying that proximity to high-voltage lines raises a child's chances of contracting leukemia by 50%—hardly a negligible figure.

While making this admission, the report goes on to emphasize that childhood leukemia is "a rare disease." This means about one case per 30,000 children in a year, says committee vice-chair David Savitz of the University of North Carolina. Since about one-quarter of homes are exposed to power lines, a bit of arithmetic shows that raising this rate by 50% could cause hundreds of additional deaths per year in the United States!

Perhaps not as frightening as destruction of the ozone layer, but far worse than some other current scares, such as passenger-side air bags. How to reconcile the headlines with the 50% increase? It seems that although statistical studies of humans demonstrate an *association* between EMF strength and cancer, laboratory research has not found the mechanism by which EMFs actually cause cancer. So while the epidemiologists believe there is a problem, the physicists [sic] don't buy it.

The report, rather than focusing on this association, instead centers on the lack of physical proof: "No clear, convincing evidence exists to show that residential exposure to electric and magnetic fields are a threat to human health." Yet in a dissenting statement three committee members point out that, "Even in the case of cigarette smoking, it took nearly 50 years after the demonstration of a statistical association with lung cancer for scientists to define a cellular mechanism by which compounds in smoke could definitely cause the cellular changes associated with lung cancer."

The report's executive summary, and chair Charles Stevens, argue that the association of power lines with cancer could be pure coincidence. Other factors, such as "age of home, housing density, and neighborhood traffic density," could be the cause of the higher rates of leukemia.

But epidemiologists say that these other factors have been investigated and no relationship has been found. "There is no good evidence to suggest that it is something else [other than EMFs]—socioeconomic status, traffic density, or the type of neighborhood," says committee member Larry Anderson of Pacific Northwest Labs. And member Daniel Driscoll of the New York State Department of Public Services agrees.

By adopting an extremely high standard of proof to reach a conclusion of "guilty" the committee ensured that it would exonerate the defendant, says Louis Slessin, editor of *Microwave News*. Stevens also used "the oldest trick in the book," by issuing a press release that did not reflect the more balanced comments in the full report, adds Slessin.

Whose interests would be threatened by a conclusion that EMFs cause leukemia? The conventional view, seconded by Larry Anderson, is that the electric utilities have the most at risk, since their power lines criss-cross the nation, entering every community.

But, claims Slessin, "We are talking about all the technologies of the 21st century. The number one interest group is the military." The modern military, he argues, is fully dependent on electromagnetic fields, for weapons, reconnaissance and communications. Physicists, such as those on the committee, whose work is heavily funded by the military, "are doing the work of the Department of Defense, either consciously or unconsciously," says Slessin.

So don't believe the reassurances from the National Academy of Sciences. Until further notice, if you can avoid living near a power line, do so. And while you're at it, stay away from military bases.

Resources: Possible Health Effects of Exposure to Residential Electric and Magnetic Fields, National Research Council (National Academy of Sciences), October, 1996; "NAS Finds No EMF-Cancer Link; Report Stirs Controversy," *Microwave News,* Nov/Dec 1996.

Marc Breslow, *Dollars and Sense,* May/June 1997

13. **Power lines not a cancer risk for children**

Children who live near high voltage power lines appear to be no more likely to get leukemia than other kids, doctors report today in the most extensive study of the controversial issue ever done.

Researchers in nine states studied 629 children with leukemia and 619 healthy children. No child was admitted to the study unless the investigators could measure the electromagnetic fields (EMF) in homes where the children had lived 70% of the time. In addition, the researchers:

• Measured EMF in all homes where children under 5 had lived more than 6 months.

• Measured the EMF in homes where the mothers of 460 children—half of whom had cancer—lived for 5 months of their pregnancy.

• Placed dose meters in the children's bedrooms for a day.

They found that children without cancer were exposed to the same levels of electromagnetic energy as children with cancer, effectively ruling out EMF as a cause.

"Overall, I believe this study demonstrates that exposure to electromagnetic fields does not increase a child's risk of leukemia," says Leslie Robinson, of the University of Minnesota and a co-author of the report in today's *New England Journal of Medicine.*

The study, sponsored by the National Cancer Institute, is the latest of hundreds to examine EMF and cancer. Parents nationwide have been alarmed and concerns have cost the nation an estimated $1 billion a year in diminished real estate prices and stalled power-transmission projects.

All of the studies, including the 1979 report that triggered these worries had drawbacks. Indeed, the National Research Council, an arm of the National Academy of Sciences, reported eight months ago that 500 studies over 17 years yielded no conclusive evidence that household EMF causes cancer.

The overall finding comes with a caveat. A handful of children exposed to moderately elevated EMF appeared to be 1.7 times more likely to develop cancer. In contrast, smokers face a 20-fold increase in cancer risk.

However, the children's risk increase was so small—14 of the 19 had cancer—that researchers believe it's a matter of chance.

Even more telling was evidence indicating that children exposed to much more powerful energy fields faced no risk.

USA TODAY, July 3, 1997

Should AIDS exhibit be OK'd as school field trip?
(Arguments 14 and 15 are from the *Las Vegas Sun,* March, 1996)

14. **Yes: Information is not false; trustees should reconsider their decision**
Sandra Thompson, managing editor of the *Las Vegas Sun*

The message is written in a teenage scrawl: "A friend of mine is always having unprotected sex. I hope she doesn't have AIDS."

One of many comments in a book at the AIDS exhibit in the Lied Discovery Children's Museum, it sums up one of the purposes of the exhibit: To inform people that if they have sex, they can get AIDS.

And that message is causing a ruckus in the community.

The School Board—without having seen the exhibit—on February 13 voted against approving it as a field trip for students. Members may reconsider their decision at a March 12 board meeting since several have seen the exhibit since their vote.

All members should see the exhibit for themselves and then approve it as a field-trip option.

The operative word here is "option."

By its vote, the School Board in effect made the decision for every parent. Critics counter that parents still have the choice—they can take their kids to the museums themselves.

Sure. And they could do other things with them, spend time with them and get involved in their education and extracurricular activities.

The reality is that many parents don't even attend their own children's school activities let alone take them to a museum.

I agree with Nevada Concerned Citizens that parents should take a more active role in their children's lives, especially education. They should know what their children are learning.

The furor over students seeing the traveling national AIDS exhibit centers on a perception that it does not stress abstinence, and talks about the risks of unprotected sex. Nevada Concerned Citizens objects to wording in the exhibit literature that says to protect yourself against AIDS, don't share needles and wear a condom during sex.

Members say that's misinformation because just doing that won't protect you, won't prevent AIDS. After all, condoms break.

The objection is based on semantics. The exhibit does not say taking such precautions will protect you 100 percent. And several times it mentions abstinence as the safest and best way to avoid AIDS.

I'm a great believer in youths abstaining from sex. But look around you: Kids are sexually active. They need information contained in the exhibit. They need to know what can happen if they fool around.

The exhibit does not promote sex. Nor does it promote a certain lifestyle connected with AIDS such as homosexuality, promiscuity or drug use.

"Whenever you deal with issues like this you set up alarms," Emily Newberry says of the "What About AIDS?" exhibit. "These are touchy issues. It's not the easiest topic to bring up."

Newberry is the public affairs coordinator for the Lied Discovery Children's Museum. She says the exhibit, which opened Feb. 3, is a national touring exhibit that does not contain any misinformation. A local advisory board of health-care professionals, educators and others reviewed the exhibit to ensure that.

"We got this exhibit because we were the only science museum in the state," she says, adding that it contains strong science content "with a compassionate side."

If school field trips were approved for the AIDS exhibit, Newberry says students would be accompanied by teachers and a school nurse who could clear up any perceived misinformation.

High school students should see the exhibit. And just because it's a field trip does not mean ALL students should attend. Parents who don't want their children to view such an exhibit should have the option to say no. Likewise, those parents who do should have the option to say yes.

15. **No: Amid questions about HIV virus, trustees were right to reject trip**
Kris Jensen of Nevada Concerned Citizens

Contrary to accusations, the School Board acted responsibly and wisely when it voted not to allow the AIDS exhibit to be a school-sponsored field trip. The five board members each had individual concerns which were all valid reasons as to why they would not endorse the AIDS exhibit and send busloads of school children to the museum.

Nevada Concerned Citizens had attended meetings and had fully reviewed the materials (all 65 pages), when finally provided in the School Board back-up material. Within the panels on display in the exhibit is a statement that we found to be untruthful and were concerned about given the fact that they were seeking permission for Clark County School District students to view this display on school time.

It reads: "*HIV is spread only by sexual intercourse, contact with blood or from a pregnant mother to her unborn child. By not sharing needles and not having sexual intercourse without a condom, we can protect ourselves from infection with HIV.*"

This is a blatant lie. Risk may be reduced, but there is no 100 percent assurance that we will be protected from infection by using a condom. What would happen when the first student who read and believed that statement contracted AIDS?

After we read this statement, we raised the concern to the School Board that this is inaccurate information and that we need to be totally honest with the students. There is no room for error in contracting AIDS, it is 100 percent fatal. We must be completely straight and say that the *only safe* way for protection from infection is abstinence. Other methods may reduce risk, but don't tell people that they are protected and imply they are safe.

Perhaps the fact that 230 million AIDS viruses can fit on the head of a pin and certain condoms allow passage should tell us that there is no fail-safe way to protect ourselves from infection with HIV other than abstinence.

Condoms leak. Perhaps the fact that dentists double and even triple glove when dealing with AIDS patients, and their actions are nowhere near as risky, should send us a message. So don't lead Clark County school kids down the primrose path with a false assurance.

Former Secretary of Education William Bennet stated: ". . . 'safe sex' or even 'safer sex' was no way to prevent AIDS, that people had to re-learn the value of traditional morality or play a dangerous game."

Dr. Theresa Cranshaw, former member of the Presidential AIDS Commission, said: "Saying that the use of condoms is 'safe sex' is in fact playing Russian roulette. A lot of people will die in this dangerous game."

What about the three women out of 18 who contracted AIDS from their husbands while using condoms during intercourse in Dr. Margaret Fischl's extensive study (that's a 17 percent failure rate)!

Best yet, there's the report how an Australian man's sperm, frozen for months at temperatures that would kill other viruses, infected four of the eight women impregnated.

The point is that the jury is still out as to the "only" methods of transmission of AIDS. Why would we put children at greater risk by telling them half-truths and giving them false assurances?

We commend the five School Board members who had a concern with misinformation that could cost a student his/her life and voted not to lend their endorsement. We encourage them to hold firm for the protection of Clark County school children.

Furthermore, we challenge the Lied Discovery Children's Museum and the National Aids Exhibit Consortium to give their patrons honest and accurate information. Don't ask the School Board to endorse false statements and contradictory information. Do not risk lives by spreading inaccurate information that could have deadly results.

Writing Lesson 15

You understand the basics of how to reason about cause and effect. And you know a lot about critical thinking and why there's a course on this subject. So write a *one page* argument either for or against the following:

"Reading this book has caused me to become a better student."

Check whether your instructor has chosen a *DIFFERENT TOPIC* for this assignment.

Writing Lesson 16

For each cartoon below there is a sentence that can be understood as a causal claim. Argue either for or against that causal claim, based on what you see in the cartoon and your common knowledge: Check that the necessary conditions for cause and effect are satisfied and that you have not made any of the common mistakes in reasoning about cause and effect.

1.

The falling apple knocked Dick unconscious.

2.

The wasps chased Professor Zzzyzzx because he hit their hive.

3.

Dick got burned because he put too much lighter fluid on the barbecue.

4.

Suzy failed because she stayed up late dancing.

Review Exercises Chapters 12–15

1. What is an argument?

2. What is the definition of "good argument"?

3. What is the difference between a valid argument and a strong argument?

4. Is every valid or strong argument with true premises good? Explain.

5. What is reasoning by analogy?

6. What are the steps in evaluating an analogy?

7. Define, for a collection of numbers:
    a. The average.

    b. The mean.

    c. The median.

    d. The mode.

8. What is a "two times zero is still zero" claim? Give an example.

9. Give an example of phony precision.

10. a. What is a generalization?

    b. What do we call the group being generalized from?

    c. What do we call the group being generalized to?

11. What is a representative sample?

12. Is every randomly chosen sample representative? Explain.

13. Is it ever possible to make a good generalization from a sample of just one?
    Explanation or example.

14. A poll says that the incumbent is preferred by 42% of the voters with a margin of error of 3% and confidence level of 97%. What does that mean?

16. What are the three premises needed for a good generalization?

17. What do we call a weak generalization from a sample that is obviously too small?

18. List the necessary conditions for there to be cause and effect.

19. What are sufficient conditions for there to be cause and effect?

20. What do we call the unstated claims necessary to establish cause and effect?

21. List three common mistakes in reasoning about causes and give an example of each.

22. List the three common types of experiments used to establish cause in populations and give an example of each.

23. Why is it better to reason well with someone even if you could convince him or her with bad arguments?

24. a. What did you find most valuable in this course?

    b. What did you find least valuable in this course?

    c. Would you recommend this course to a friend? Why?

Writing Lesson 17

Let's see how much you've learned in this course. Write an argument for or against the following:

"Student athletes should be given special leniency when the instructor assigns course marks."

Using Examples in Reasoning

Exercises for Using Examples

1. Detail how examples were used in making the definition of "argument" in Chapter 1 (look at the three reasons for making examples with definitions).

2. Define "professional athlete." Use examples to contrast professional athletes with college athletes who receive scholarships and amateur athletes who are supported by governments to participate in the Olympics.

3. Define "school cafeteria" and use examples to show that you've got the definition right.

4. Define "student financial aid," and use examples to make your definition clear.

5. Detail how examples were used in Chapter 4 to show how to use the Guide to Repairing Arguments.

6. Show the following are false or at least dubious:
   a. All dogs bark.

   b. All cats kill songbirds.

   c. Nearly everyone who's at this college is on financial aid.

   d. No teacher at this university gives good lectures.

   e. No fast-food restaurant serves healthy food.

7. Say "preposterous" ten times. Does it begin to sound like a nonsense word?

For each argument below, if it is meant to be valid but is invalid, give an example to show that. If it's meant to be strong but it's weak, give enough examples to show that. If the argument is valid but not good, give an example to show why.

8. All good teachers give fair exams. Dr. Zzzyzzx gives fair exams. So Dr. Zzzyzzx is a good teacher.

9. If this course were easy, the exams would be fair. The exams are fair. So this course is easy.

10. President Clinton didn't inhale marijuana. So President Clinton never got high from marijuana.

11. Almost all teachers at this school speak English as their first language. So your instructor speaks English as his or her first language.

12. Dr. Zzzyzzx was late for class. He's never been late for class before. He's always conscientious in all his duties. So he must have been in an accident.

Diagramming

Exercises for Section A

Diagram the following arguments. Repair the arguments as necessary.

1. Dr. E is a teacher. All teachers are men. So Dr. E is a man.

2. No one under sixteen has a driver's license. So Zoe must be at least sixteen.

3. Sheep are the dumbest animals. If the one in front walks off a cliff, all the rest will follow him. And if they get rolled over on their backs, they can't right themselves.

4. I'm on my way to school. I left five minutes late. Traffic is heavy. Therefore, I'll be late for class. So I might as well stop and get breakfast.

5. Pigs are very intelligent animals. They make great pets. They learn to do tricks as well as any dog can. They can be housetrained, too. And they are affectionate, since they like to cuddle. Pigs are known as one of the smartest animals there are. And if you get bored with them or they become unruly, you can eat them.

6. Smoking is disgusting. It makes your breath smell horrid. If you've ever kissed someone after they smoked a cigarette you feel as though you're going to vomit. Besides, it will kill you.

7. You're good at numbers. You sort of like business. You should major in accounting—accountants make really good money.

8. Inherited property such as real estate, stocks, bonds, etc. is given a fresh start basis when inherited. That is, for purposes of future capital gains tax computations, it is treated as though it were purchased at its market value at the time of inheritance. Thus, when you sell property which was acquired by inheritance, tax is due only on the appreciation in value since the time it was inherited. No tax is ever paid on the increase in value that took place when the property belonged to the previous owner.

1994 Tax Guide for College Teachers

Exercises for Section B

Diagram and evaluate the following arguments:

1. You should not take illegal drugs. They can kill you. If you overdose, you can die. If you share a needle, you could get AIDS and then die. If you don't die, you may end up a vegetable or otherwise permanently incapacitated. Using drugs runs the risk of getting arrested and possibly going to jail. Or at least having a hefty fine against you. Although some think the "high" from drugs is worth all the risks, the truth is that they are addicted and are only trying to justify supporting their habit.

2. Zoe: I think sex is the answer to almost everyone's problems.

   Dick: How can you say that?

   Zoe: It takes away your tensions, right?

   Dick: Not if you're involved with someone you don't like.

   Zoe: Well, anyway, it makes you feel better.

   Dick: Not if it's against your morals. Anyway, heroin makes you feel good, too.

   Zoe: But it's healthy, natural, just like eating and drinking.

   Dick: Sure, and you can catch terrible diseases. Sex should be confined to marriage.

   Zoe: Is that a proposal?

3. Dick: Nixon was a crook.

    Zoe: No he wasn't. Remember that famous "Checkers" speech where he said so?

    Dick: That was just political evasion. Anyway, you can't just take someone's word that he's not a criminal, especially if he's a politician. He directed the break-in at the Democratic Party Headquarters.

    Zoe: They never showed that he did that.

    Dick: That's because his accomplices like Haldemann were covering up. That's why they got pardoned. And he used the FBI against his enemies. He was a criminal. It was stupid for Clinton to make a speech honoring him when he died.

    Zoe: Maybe Clinton was doing it so that when he dies someone will make a speech for him, too

Truth-Tables

Key Words   classical abstraction   conjunction
                 truth-table   negation
                 ∧   disjunction
                 ⌐   conditional
                 ∨   tautology
                 →   valid argument form

Exercises for Sections A and B

1. What are the four fundamental English words or phrases that we will analyze in studying compound claims?

2. What is the first big assumption about claims we made (the Classical Abstraction) when we decided to use the symbols ∧, ∨, ⌐, → ?

3. Explain why using symbols makes you nervous. Suggest a way you can overcome your distaste for them. (If they don't make you nervous, answer this question for your classmates who are bothered by them.)

4. What is a tautology?

5. What is the method for checking whether a claim is a tautology?

6. Explain the method for checking if two forms of claims are equivalent.

Here's an example of a way Tom devised to check whether a claim is a tautology. It's a little long-winded, but it made it clear to him.

Decide whether   (A ∧ B) → ¬(A ∨ B) is a tautology.

A	B		A	∧	B		¬	(A	∨	B)		(A∧B)	→	¬(A∨B)
T	T		T	T	T		F	T	T	T		T	F	F
T	F		T	F	F		F	T	T	F		F	T	F
F	T		F	F	T		F	F	T	T		F	T	F
F	F		F	F	F		T	F	F	F		F	T	T
1	2		3	4	5		6	7	8	9		10	11	12

Columns 1 and 2 are all the possible combinations of truth-values of the claims.
Columns 3 and 5 are just 1 and 2 repeated to see how to get column 4
    (it's the table for A ∧ B).
Columns 7 and 9 are just 1 and 2 repeated so as to see how to get column 8
    (it's the table for A ∨ B).
Then column 6 is the table for ¬ applied to column 8, which gives the truth-
    values of ¬(A ∨ B).
Column 10 is just column 4 repeated. And column 12 is just column 6 again.
    That lets us see how to get column 11 using the table for →.
Column 11 gives the truth-values for (A ∧ B)→¬(A ∨ B). Since there's an F in
that column, this isn't the form of a tautology.

Use the truth-table method to show that the following are tautologies:

7. ¬¬A → A

8. ¬(A ∧ ¬A)

9. $((A \rightarrow B) \wedge (\neg A \rightarrow B)) \rightarrow B$

10. $\neg (A \wedge B) \rightarrow (\neg A \vee \neg B)$

Decide whether the following are tautologies by the truth-table method. Then explain why in your own words.

11. $A \rightarrow (A \vee B)$

12. $((A \vee B) \wedge \neg B) \rightarrow A$

13. $(A \vee B) \rightarrow (A \wedge B)$

14. $((A \rightarrow B) \wedge \neg B) \rightarrow \neg A$

15. $(\neg(A \wedge B) \wedge \neg A) \rightarrow B$

16. $((A \rightarrow B) \wedge (\neg A \rightarrow C)) \rightarrow (B \vee C)$

Show that the following are equivalent.

17. $\neg(A \rightarrow B)$ is the same as $A \wedge \neg B$

18. $A \rightarrow B$ is the same as $\neg A \vee B$

19. $\neg(A \wedge B)$ is the same as $\neg A \vee \neg B$

20. $\neg(A \vee B)$ is the same as $\neg A \wedge \neg B$

Exercises for Section C

1. Make up the table for $(A \vee B) \wedge \neg(A \wedge B)$ and show that it is true when exactly one of A is true or B is true.

For each of the following, either represent it using $\wedge$, $\vee$, $\neg$, $\rightarrow$, or explain why it can't be represented.

2. If critical thinking is hard, then mathematics is impossible.

3. If you don't apologize, I'll never talk to you again.

4. Dick prefers steak, while Zoe prefers spaghetti.

5. Dick was shaving while Zoe was preparing dinner.

6. Either Dick loves Zoe best, or he loves Spot best.

7. Even if you do whine all the time, I love you.

8. Spot is a good dog even though he scared the living bejabbers out of your cat.

9. Spot is a good dog because he scared the living bejabbers out of your cat.

10. We're going to go to the movies or go out for dinner tonight.

11. Since 2 + 2 is 4, and 4 times 2 is 8, I should be ahead $8, not $7, in blackjack.

12. If Dick has a class and Zoe is working, there's no point in calling their home to ask them over for dinner.

13. If it's really true that if Dick takes Spot for a walk he'll do the dishes, then Dick won't take Spot for a walk.

14. If Dick goes to the basketball game, then he either got a free ticket or he borrowed money from somebody.

15. Either we'll go to the movies or visit your mom if I get home from work by 6.

16. Whenever Spot barks like that, there's a skunk or racoon in the yard.

17. I'm not going to visit your mother and I'm not going to do the dishes, regardless of whether you get mad at me or try to cajole me.

18. Every student in Dr. E's class is over 18 or is taking the course while in high school.

19. No matter whether the movie gets out early or late, we're going to go out for pizza.

20. Suggest ways to represent:
    a. A only if B
    b. A unless B
    c. When A, B
    d. A if and only if B
    e. B just in case A
    f. Neither A nor B

Exercises for Section D

1. What does it mean to say an argument form is valid?

2. If an argument has a form that is not valid, is it necessarily a bad argument?

Use truth-tables to decide whether the following argument forms are valid.

3. $\dfrac{A \rightarrow B, \ B}{A}$

4. $\dfrac{A \rightarrow B, \ A \rightarrow \neg B}{\neg A}$

5. $\dfrac{A, \ \neg A}{B}$

6. $\dfrac{A \vee B}{A \wedge B}$

7. $\dfrac{A \vee B, \ \neg A}{B}$

8. $\dfrac{B \vee D, \ B \rightarrow C, \ D \rightarrow E}{C \vee E}$

9. $\dfrac{A \to \neg B, \ B \wedge \neg C}{A \to C}$

10. $\dfrac{A \to \neg\neg B, \ \neg C \vee A, \ C}{B}$

Represent the arguments in Exercises 11–17 and decide whether they are valid. Use truth-tables or not as you wish.

11. If Spot is a cat, then Spot meows. Spot is not a cat. So Spot doesn't meow.

12. Either the moon is made of green cheese or $2 + 2 = 4$. But the moon is not made of green cheese. So $2 + 2 = 4$.

13. Either the moon is made of green cheese or $2 + 2 = 5$. But the moon is not made of green cheese. So $2 + 2 = 5$.

14. The students are happy if and only if no test is given. If the students are happy, the professor feels good. But if the professor feels good, he won't feel like lecturing, and if he doesn't feel like lecturing, he'll give a test. So the students aren't happy.

15. If Dick and Zoe visit his family at Christmas, then they will fly. If Dick and Zoe visit Zoe's mother at Christmas, then they will fly. But Dick and Zoe have to visit his family or her mother. So Dick and Zoe will travel by plane.

16. Tom is not from New York or Virginia. But Tom is from the East Coast. If Tom is from Syracuse, he is from New York or Virginia. So Tom is not from Syracuse.

17. The government is going to spend less on health and welfare. If the government is going to spend less on health and welfare, then either the government is going to cut the Medicare budget or the government is going to slash spending on housing. If the government is going to cut the Medicare budget, the elderly will protest. If the government is going to slash spending on housing, then advocates of the poor will protest. So the elderly will protest or advocates of the poor will protest.

Writing Lesson X

For each of the following write the best argument you can that has as conclusion the claim below the cartoon. List only the premises and conclusion. If you believe the best argument is only weak, explain why.

Do not make up a story about the cartoon. Use what you see in the cartoon and your common knowledge.

1.

Spot made the boy go away.

2.

The professor is boring.

3.

Spot took the steak.

4.

Flo isn't really sick.

5.

The fellow standing between Harry and Manuel is or was in the military.

6.

Dick shouldn't get a haircut here.

7.

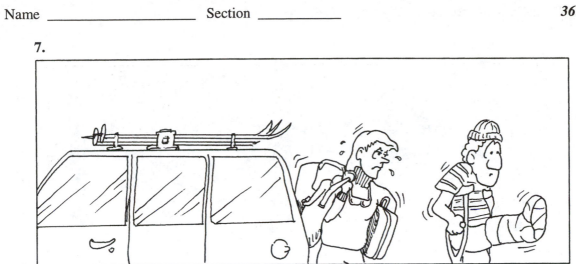

Dick broke his leg skiing.

8.

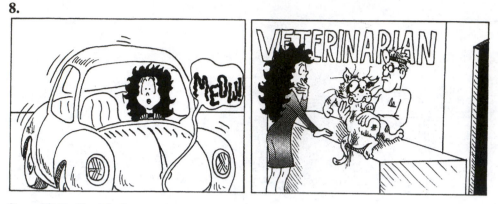

Suzy hit Puff with the car.

9.

Spot is afraid of being punished.

Causal Claims

For each cartoon below there is a sentence that can be understood as a causal claim. Argue either for or against that causal claim, based on what you see in the cartoon and your common knowledge: Check that the necessary conditions for cause and effect are satisfied and that you have not made any of the common mistakes in reasoning about cause and effect.

10.

Dick had to hitchhike because he didn't get gas.

11.

The cat made Spot run away.

12.

Dick crashed because of the turtle.

The End